SHADOWS ON THE GULF

SHADOWS ON THE GULF

A Journey Through Our Last Great Wetland

Rowan Jacobsen

BLOOMSBURY

New York   Berlin   London   Sydney

Published by Bloomsbury USA, New York

All papers used by Bloomsbury USA are natural, recyclable products made
from wood grown in well-managed forests. The manufacturing processes
conform to the environmental regulations of the country of origin.

Library of Congress Cataloging-in-Publication Data

Jacobsen, Rowan.
Shadows on the Gulf : a journey through our last great wetland /
Rowan Jacobsen.
p. cm.
ISBN 978-1-60819-581-7 (hardback)
1. Natural history—Mexico, Gulf of.   2. Coastal ecology—Mexico,
Gulf of.   3. Mexico, Gulf of.   4. Natural history—Gulf Coast (U.S.)
5. Coastal ecology—Gulf Coast (U.S.)   6. Gulf Coast (U.S.)   I. Title.
QH92.3.J33 2011
508.76—dc22
2010051498

First U.S. edition 2011

1   3   5   7   9   10   8   6   4   2

Typeset by Westchester Book Group
Printed in the U.S.A. by Quad/Graphics, Fairfield, Pennsylvania

When we try to pick out anything by itself,
we find it hitched to everything else
in the Universe.

—JOHN MUIR

CONTENTS

Chapter 1

FALLING FOR THE GULF

IN THE TIDE pools of Alabama's Grand Bay National Wildlife Refuge, on May 13, 2010, the water was alive and blue.
"Look at that turquoise!" said Bill Finch, director of conservation for the Alabama chapter of the Nature Conservancy. "Look
at it!" We were standing in a salt marsh in Grand Bay, crown
jewel of Gulf natural areas, and squinting into a depression in the
rushes. I leaned in close to watch an aquamarine trail streaking
through the water like a shooting star. "Look at that turquoise!"
Bill said again. "Isn't it beautiful? How do I capture that on film
someday?"

We were watching male sailfin mollies. The minnow-size fish
live close to shore and move into open pools in the rushes, where
they can display for females without being eaten, turning sideways and making quick runs across the tide pool, catching the
sun along special iridescent scales. It looked like they were flash-
ing neon lights. "God, that's stunning," Bill said. "I could watch
all day."

It was springtime on the Gulf Coast—mating season. All
around us, life was making new life, or at least contemplating

the idea. The male sailfin mollies were nudging females toward the privacy of the reeds. Behind us on the salt pan, willets were flitting into the air and piping their pennywhistle love songs. A rail had just hatched her chicks in the cordgrass. At the edge of the marsh, acres of oysters were spawning. And farther out to sea, uncountable crab eggs were riding the warm Gulf currents. This was, normally, the most hopeful time of the year. And Grand Bay sure as hell looked normal. Miles of rush stretched to the Mississippi state line, backed by a wall of some of the only tidal pine forest on Earth. The sun glinted off waves rolling over vast seagrass beds. Beautiful.

But we couldn't enjoy it. If Bill wanted to capture the mollies on film, he had better do it today. Ten miles straight offshore from us, the first black cannonade of tar balls was splatting into Dauphin Island, the sandy barrier island that is the coast's first line of defense. Farther out, something dark and dead was gathering in the depths.

To the east, on the hazy horizon, we could just make out the buildings of Bayou La Batre, a small town that is America's shrimp capital. In the movie, Forrest Gump keeps his shrimp boat in Bayou La Batre. The previous weekend the town had held the Blessing of the Fleet, the traditional opening of the fishing season. The decorated boats paraded past a priest, who blessed each in turn. But then, instead of heading to sea, the boats turned around and returned to their berths. No fishing on the Gulf.

"I hope I have more time with Grand Bay," Bill said. With his gray beard, balding pate, and general demeanor, he gave the impression of being the Lorax of the coast—an impression strengthened when he later leaped across the marsh, through knee-deep muck, to stop an airboat from plowing into the needle rush. Bill has sun-reddened skin and the kind of soft Southern drawl that has always put me at ease. Today, though, the softness of his voice made the alarming nature of his words stand out almost unbearably. "I don't know that you will ever, ever see a salt pan like this anywhere else. Grand Bay is our model. If we want to know what the coast was like, we come to Grand Bay. There are all these community types, like this tidal pine forest, that just don't exist anywhere else anymore. This is just the very edge. You have to see the seagrass beds. You have to see the shell mounds." Not long ago, Bill had been out on those Native American shell mounds, on islands in the middle of the bay, shucking oysters straight out of the water and picking wolfberries—North American goji berries, delicious savory little fruits that grow on the mounds—and grazing on glasswort, a salty, crunchy, asparagus-like plant. "It's the way people must have eaten for ten thousand years."

In early April, the Nature Conservancy's Alabama chapter had established a mile and a half of new oyster reef on Coffee Island, off the Alabama coast. It was the best oyster-restoration project this country had ever seen. It had seemed like a heartening success until the Macondo well beneath the *Deepwater Horizon* blew out on April 20 and sent a tidal wave of oil straight toward that reef. I'd been interested in reef restoration for years and decided to visit those oysters a few days before the oil did. Bill and I got talking, and at every turn in the conversation he told me something new and surprising. Alabama has the greatest biodiversity of any state east of the Mississippi. Alabama has the greatest diversity of crawfish. Of freshwater fish and mussels. It has the greatest concentration of turtle species in the *world*. The entire Appalachian Mountain chain has twelve species of oak trees; Alabama has thirty-nine. I felt the scales of ignorance falling from my eyes.

Sensing a kindred spirit, Bill had brought me to Grand Bay, to see it as it was, before anything changed. He'd been coming here since he was a kid growing up in southern Mississippi in an old Choctaw town. "In those days, it was just the scenery of growing up. I don't want to say you take it for granted, but you don't have a context for it." Now he had a context. "You can imagine what happens when oil runs into this. It's just gonna stick to it. It's the gum-in-the-hair problem. You'll never get it out. But here's the real problem. It's gonna be coming in for a very long time, and some of it's gonna be coming in on storm tides. If we were to get a storm tide that lifted it right over this marsh, that would really worry me."

It was only a few weeks after the blowout, but already it was clear that the thickest, tarriest oil—the stuff riding well beneath the surface—would be coming in sporadically for years. When oil hits marshes, it chokes out the oxygen and nitrogen that the grasses need. The soil goes hypoxic. Then the marsh grass dies. Estuaries like Grand Bay are where 90 percent of the fish species in the Gulf come to breed. They are the nurseries of the Gulf. Whenever an acre of marsh grass dies, another acre of the Gulf dies.

"We don't really know what breeds in these tide pools," Bill said. "The young come in here for protection. There's a real convergence of freshwater and saltwater species." In 2004, when Bill was an editor at the Mobile Press-Register, the reporter Ben Raines discovered a possum pipefish in Grand Bay, the only one seen in the Gulf in more than thirty years. The find scuttled an oil company's plan to drill for natural gas right in the heart of Grand Bay, which has the best remaining seagrass meadows possum pipefish require. "It was found only in these types of habitats," Bill explained. "And now it may be too late." Bill turned away from watching the mollies and stared out at the waves. He was speaking softly, as if to himself. "I fall in love with these places way too easy."

Our species has always hugged the coasts whenever it could. Not only because we like gazing out at the rolling waves and the sea of infinite mystery and possibilities beyond, but also because the coasts of the world are uniquely abundant in everything that makes our lives grand. The zone where land and sea intertwine has an intensity to it, like the embrace of two living bodies. We all pick up on that feeling—a quickening of the senses, an intuition that vital things are happening.

And we're right. In the places where land and sea come together in a tangle of limbs, new life begins—life that couldn't exist without the unique contributions of both partners. The sea provides the watery medium, and the land provides the fertility. That's why the best grazing in the ocean is in the wetlands—the shallow, warm, protected estuaries. There, in the bays and marshes, seagrasses and algae thrive, and everything that eats greens, or that eats the things that eat those greens, comes to the table.

You'd think that we'd place an extraordinarily high value on such places. After all, we have made our livelihoods off their largesse for millennia. And it isn't simply a matter of livelihoods. It's a question of meaning, and beauty, and spirit. They are the places where, like the old beer commercial, you look around at your buddies and say, "It doesn't get any better than this." This was not lost on the first Native American residents of the region, whose vast oyster shell middens remain as silent witness to their coastal devotion. Nor was it lost on the first European arrivals, refugees from Acadia and frontier types from France and Spain, who mingled to form a unique culture powered by everything that was bountiful on the bayous.

I first fell in love with the Gulf of Mexico twenty-five years ago, during four years of college in Sarasota, Florida. From the cradle of a giant banyan tree near College Hall, I'd watch a ginger sun sink into the silvery bay. My friends and I would slip away to Lido Beach for midnight swims. We'd pad through the mucky estuaries, on alert for horseshoe crabs and stingrays, then later sit cross-legged back at campus with a pile of Apalachicola oysters, a couple of knives, and a cold, cheap six-pack. And now I was back, to see it once again before two hundred million gallons of oil, and a heavy-handed response to that crude, altered it in ways I couldn't anticipate.

Perhaps because the centers of political and cultural power lie on our Atlantic and Pacific coasts, the Gulf Coast has never gotten its due. It's off most people's radar, except perhaps as the "Redneck Riviera." Most never learn about the other Gulf, the natural miracle with the finest beaches in the nation, the best diving, the best birding, the most productive wetlands.

The Gulf Coast will surprise you. If you're used to the Atlantic or Pacific coasts, your first reaction to the Gulf is to melt a little. The sand is so fine, the water so warm, the waves so gentle. It seems like the world's biggest kiddie pool. If history had been different, it would have become the globe's elite beach playground. A few spots on the Gulf are like that. But the rest went down a different path.

On Dauphin Island, Alabama, I slipped out of the Pelican Pub, where an out-of-work charter boat captain in an XXL teal sportfishing shirt had had enough of out-of-towners like me ("Tar balls on the beach is normal! Dead sea turtles is normal! People need to understand, this is all normal!"), and walked the baby-powder beach. Little girls in bikinis splashed and giggled in the shallows and tried to stay out of the way of teams in hard hats and protective white jumpsuits patrolling for tar balls. A quarter mile down the beach, hundreds of dead catfish were washing ashore. I stood there, waves lapping my toes. And then my eyes caught something blocky on the horizon. Once I adjusted to the shimmering waterline, I could see the distant rigs—five, six, eight of them— rising out of the Gulf on spindly legs, like the Martian death machines in *War of the Worlds*.

This is no eulogy for the Gulf. Resist the media's hysteria to write off the whole area. The Gulf lives—for now. When I told people in the Northeast and Northwest during the summer of 2010 that I'd just returned from a few weeks in the Gulf, they looked at me as if I'd just crawled out of a foxhole in Afghanistan. "Oh my God," they'd say, sympathy in their eyes, "was the stench unbearable?"

In places, yes. The ugliest slick I saw was at Grand Isle, Louisiana. The beach was closed for mile after mile, blocked off with plastic orange construction screen. Signs on the road advertised ON-SITE DISASTER RELIEF CATERING. At the far end of the island, at Grand Isle State Park, I found a young ranger named Leanne Sarco quietly scrubbing oil from one hermit crab after another with a Q-tip. Leanne was wearing white slacks, shirt, and cowboy boots and was smeared with oil from her boots to her blond hair. She led me along a path to the last wild beach on the island, a magnet for birds and other wildlife. Liquid crude rippled in the tide pools. The sand was the color of coffee grounds. When you squeezed a handful, gobs of black jelly oozed out between your fingers. Leanne told me that the oil had seeped several feet below the surface and would be bubbling up for years.

Horrible. A tragedy that never should have happened. But I had driven through a hundred miles of gorgeous marsh to get to that spot—marsh that the press ignored. One captain participating in BP's Vessels of Opportunity oil-recovery program in Alabama was disgusted with the media coverage. "They don't come down here and take a ride in Mobile Bay and cover two or three hundred square miles and take pictures of how pretty things are," he told me. "They sit on their asses until somebody reports an oiled bird, and then they take six hundred pictures of it."

That was my impression, too. It's not really the fault of the press, whose job is to find the most riveting stories and images. But then people take these extreme cases and mentally paint the whole Gulf Coast with them. That's not the reality. Most of the Gulf Coast has not been touched by the oil spill and is as beautiful and vital as ever. I spent the majority of my time on the Gulf Coast traveling through a paradise of pompano, waterfowl, and incredibly friendly and good-humored people. As long as I stayed away from Interstate 10, I had no issues with diesel fumes. The scents I recall most vividly are those of salt air, oyster shells, and Vietnamese pho.

Make no mistake, the Gulf Coast has been horribly impacted by the *Deepwater Horizon* oil spill—some of it directly, most of it indirectly. It will take years for some of that damage to come to light. But in a way, BP's blowout simply brought some old, hidden issues into plain sight. "We were headed for trouble anyway in ten to fifteen years," said Bill Finch, who calls the BP oil spill "merely the latest in a hundred-year catastrophe along the Gulf Coast. Now we've just shortened that timetable. If we use this as an occasion to turn away from all the shit we've been doing all these years, it'd be great. But if we keep on doing what we've been doing, and have the oil on top of that . . ."

This book is not simply about the *Deepwater Horizon* oil spill. That disaster is just one piece in a terribly disturbing overall trend of lives ruined, environments trashed, places bled of character until they are pale and placeless. My hope is that, by painting a sort of cubist portrait of a beautiful and sometimes contradictory region, this book will let you see the Gulf as I saw it in the aftermath of the oil spill. I hope I can serve as a stand-in for the many people whose relationship to the Gulf is something like mine was: I knew it a little, liked it, harbored a few illusions about it, grew deeply concerned as the oil well churned day after day, and became amazed as I learned more about the region and its vast importance, to all of our lives, and about the unbelievable things happening to it.

As tragic as it was, perhaps the *Deepwater Horizon* blowout can ultimately inspire more appreciation for this jewel in our backyard. If so, this disaster may still, in the long run, end up saving more livelihoods and wetlands than it destroyed. I hope that, like me, the more you learn, the more you'll agree that a national effort to restore this coast is in all of our interests. I hope you'll fall for this place, too.

Chapter 2

THE LAST HUNTER-GATHERERS
IN AMERICA

I N D U L A C , L O U I S I A N A , I stepped out of Schmoopy's Restaurant onto an oyster-shell parking lot. After the wintry
air-conditioning of the restaurant, the steamy Louisiana air hit
me like a moist towel upside the head. I'd just feasted on gener-
ous piles of briny oysters and sweet shrimp, topped off with
something called a crawfish pistolette, which is kind of like
a battered, deep-fried lobster roll and is probably something
one shouldn't eat every day. It was damn good. The oysters and
shrimp were unloaded off a boat directly onto this parking lot,
then carried into Schmoopy's. ("Schmoopy" is what owner Ronnie Richaud calls his wife, and it's what she calls him.) The crawfish came from farther north, because crawfish live in freshwater
swamps, and Dulac has been taken over by saltwater.

On one side of the parking lot was Route 57 and a line of
trailer homes raised up on eleven-foot wooden pilings. On the
other side was Bayou Grand Caillou and a line of shrimp boats
paralleling the road out of sight. Beyond the road and the bayou
there was nothing but marsh grass, the flattest landscape imag-
inable, a prairie on the water. This is the landscape of the Mis-

sissippi River Delta: a bayou, a road, a line of houses on stilts, then the marsh. The design is not arbitrary. The houses are there because the bayou is there. The road, too, is there because of the bayou. It could not have been built anywhere else. Even the marshes owe their existence to the bayou. This is the inescapable logic of the delta. Everything takes its cue from the nature of the place. Everything has a reason.

A bayou is not, as many people think, a swamp. Nor is it a bay. It's a tidal river, and most of the bayous in the Mississippi River Delta were once distributaries of the Mississippi River. (A distributary is the opposite of a tributary.) As the Mississippi River reaches the flat and muddy delta—a sea-level wetland made with its own sediment—numerous distributaries branch out, and then keep branching into a many-limbed "tree" that meets the Gulf of Mexico on either side of the river's main stem. These are the bayous of the delta. Slowly fed by the Mississippi when it was high, they used to meander to the Gulf, taking their own sweet time. They also used to flood regularly, along with the Mississippi. When they did so, the first place they deposited their mud was on their immediate banks. Smaller, lighter sediment was spread out through the marshes. Over thousands of years, this resulted in two strips of high ground—and by "high ground," I mean just a few feet above sea level—lining each of the bayous. When the Cajuns and others colonized this land, starting in the 1760s, these levees, the only terra firma for hundreds of square miles, were naturally where they settled. They accessed stores, churches, and each other by boat and worked the marshes for shrimp, oysters, crabs, and fish. The slow-moving bayous became the roads of these linear communities.

In some ways, not much has changed. "Around here," Captain Wendy Billiot, my lunch companion, had told me, "people don't say the name of the town they live in; they say the name of the bayou they live on. And we don't have north, south, east, and west. We have down the bayou, up the bayou, and across the bayou." Most of the travel these days is done by car, on the roads that hug the bayous, but the communities are still linear, and every household still keeps a boat on the bayou. One such waterway, Bayou Lafourche, is often called "the longest Main Street in the world," sixty-five miles of taffy-stretched small town.

I fall in love with these places way too easy, too. I guess you could call them places that are still places: places you couldn't mistake for anywhere else. To me, heaven is venturing somewhere completely new and getting a sense of the patterns of existence that have formed it. The way that climate, topography, and plants and animals have come together to create a unique environment, and the way that people through the centuries have adapted to it, spinning a culture out of those raw materials. This is why we travel. We're hungry for authenticity. When in New Orleans, we eat gumbo and crawfish étouffée and drink chicory coffee. We want to participate, even if only briefly, in the daily rhythms of a place—to play at being a local.

It's no wonder why. Most of us have no such landmarks to guide us. Authenticity is often hard to come by in America. There are no more elm trees on Elm Street. There's no view from Bella Vista. There's just the vertigo of having so little solid meaning in the land beneath our feet.

Not so in the Mississippi River Delta. There, and in many other wetlands along the Gulf Coast, lives are still finely tuned to place. The things people do for work and fun are directly linked to the world-class wetland on their doorstep. That's inspiring, and great fun to be a part of, but it's also scary as hell, because the rhythms of the Gulf Coast are falling apart.

Since the blowout, the lunch crowd in Schmoopy's had been only half of what it should be. While I had eaten my lunch, Ronnie Richaud had spent most of his time shaking his head and consulting the latest maps of fishing closures from the Louisiana Department of Wildlife and Fisheries. "We surrounded," he'd said. "I figure we got about two days. There's a joke goin' round you won't need no oil on your fish. Puttin' me some oysters away from the oyster boat next door. He's pretty much to the end, too. He didn't step it up." Oystermen spend half their time traveling to and from the oyster grounds, and Ronnie had suggested that they start sleeping on their boats at the grounds in one final, mad push to get the oysters before the oil arrived. He'd pointed at my notepad. "Dude, I'm just a dumb coon-ass, but you tell 'em Schmoopy says it's a good idea."

From Schmoopy's, Wendy and I drove down the road looking to buy shrimp off one of the shrimp boats moored alongside the road. Normally, this would be a simple task. Most shrimpers like to sell direct, because Asian farmed shrimp (which supplies 90 percent of the U.S. market) has driven the wholesale price so low. "Last year was a really bad year," Wendy told me. "The shrimpers get everything ready, they gas up their boats and go shrimping, because it's all they know to do, and they come back not knowing if they're even going to be able to pay for the fuel and the ice, much less support their families. We actually had neighbor striking against neighbor. The shrimpers were up in arms against the buyers. They wouldn't sell them their catch. They were selling straight off the boat because they could get two dollars a pound instead of seventy-five cents."

Now, oil from the *Deepwater Horizon* was creeping closer to Dulac. The shadow of that oil was darkening the waters only about three miles away. All the local areas in Terrebonne Parish were closed to shrimping. That had Wendy pretty freaked out. "You have to understand the cycle of life in the bayou," she said. "Right now, if this catastrophe hadn't happened, everyone would be hustling about getting ready for brown shrimp season. That lasts about six weeks, then there's a little break. Everyone fixes up their boats and gets ready for white shrimp season in August. Then September is the wild alligator harvest. Then winter is trapping, which doesn't happen very much anymore. People might do some crabbing. If you oyster, that's pretty much all you do. Then in spring, people would plant their gardens and get ready for brown shrimp season. No matter how tough times are, we can always find something to eat here."

Bayou people were locavores before locavore was cool. They're the last real hunter-gatherers in America, and they have just been clobbered by BP. Because of the spill, the state opened the shrimping season, which usually begins May 15, a few days early to give shrimpers a chance to make a little bit of income before it closed the waters, probably for the entire season. Wendy was hoping to stock up her freezer while she could. We finally managed to buy a cooler of shrimp—forty pounds for one hundred dollars—off the boat of a forty-five-year-old Cajun shrimper she knew named Kevin Lirette. Kevin wasn't thrilled with the shrimp, which are graded on how many it takes to make a pound. The lower the count, the bigger the shrimp and the higher the price. "These are 36–40s. We expect 15–20s, 21–25s. They didn't let 'em grow." He was not in a good mood, because he knew he wouldn't be making another trip for some time. "I'm worried," he said. "Now's the time we make our money. I been doing this since I was fifteen years old. I used to be on a double rig with my dad. This all I ever did do. I owe on everything I have. I don't know what I'm gonna do."

As we drove away, Wendy choked back tears. "I'm trying to stay optimistic," she said. "I'm trying to avoid the gloom and doom. But if we get oil in the marshes, that'll be the end of making a living here. If we can't shrimp, and we can't catch crabs, and we can't harvest oysters, and we can't fish, either commercial or sport, then what do we have left? The majority of these people never finished high school. What else are they gonna do? Bayou people can't pick up and do what they do anywhere else. There's a culture and a way of life here that *deserves* to exist."

Wendy discovered that way of life thirty-two years ago, when she came down from Bossier City in northern Louisiana. "It was so different down here," she remembered. "I had no clue. I thought sugarcane was skinny corn!" She worked as a roustabout on a production dock in Dulac, servicing the oil boats that serviced the rigs. "I liked it. It was good money." Then she met her future husband, a local Houma Indian who had left the shrimp boats to pilot a crew boat servicing the oil rigs. "The local women instantly hated me. I didn't belong here. I had blond hair and green eyes. I think they assumed *I'd* be prejudiced." But she eventually earned their trust. "I fell in love with the place and the people and the culture. The long, strong tendrils reached out and wouldn't let me go."

Wendy raised a daughter and four sons in the bayou. Two of the sons are in high school. The older two, like their dad and many others, moved from shrimp boats to the oil industry. "It's not a far jump from running a shrimp boat to running an oil field crew boat or work boat," Wendy explained. "Those shrimpers know the waters like the back of their hand. The oil companies were well served to get them to cross over. The oil industry has exacerbated the wetlands loss here, which has affected the fisheries, but it also becomes the hand that feeds." Her sons are tankermen on petroleum barges. "They go up and down the canals, back and forth. They don't really want to work that lifestyle, but once you start making that money, you never go back."

The region's complicated relationship with oil is perfectly captured in the fact that the bayou's Shrimp Festival, celebrated every September since 1936, officially changed its name to the Shrimp and Petroleum Festival in 1967. Oil may be what threatens the Gulf Coast, but this isn't necessarily a region that wants to be saved from it—or anything else.

From the way the press rhapsodized about southern Louisiana in the days after the spill, you'd think the region had been one long, golden tableau of gumbo joints, zydeco music, and noble fishermen working their nets. That all exists, but other parts of the Gulf Coast fully live up to the Redneck Riviera reputation, with the ugliest casinos, condos, and refineries known to humankind. In southern Louisiana, a seemingly endless number of signs advertise exotic dancers and female oil wrestling, often in what look to be convenience stores. Driving along the bayou, I saw a hand-scrawled sign advertising SHRIMP FOR SELL and another, custom printed, that said WILL REMOVE HONEYBEES FROM RESIDENT. The letters on one store's signboard proudly proclaimed OBAMA IS PROOF A VILLAGE IN KENYA IS MISSING ITS IDIOT. Barack Obama is not popular in these parts. Ronnie Richaud's main criticism of him was that, unlike Bush, he "appointed people he don't even *know* into positions of power!" Corruption and cronyism are so deeply ingrained in Louisiana that they don't even seem noteworthy after a while. That has allowed the oil industry to rule the place for decades, and that catastrophe is as much a part of the story of the region's degradation as is the *Deepwater Horizon* blowout.

After Wendy dropped the shrimp in her freezer, she said she wanted to show me something. She drove across Falgout Canal Road—the only "across the bayou" road in these parts, built on dredged material—and pulled over beside what looked to me like a typical salt marsh scene: clumps of bright green cordgrass laced with fingers of open blue water.

"Do you see?" she asked me.

I didn't. She pointed out the bleached spires of hundreds of dead tree trunks sticking out of the marsh like old, giant fence posts. "This is a dead cypress swamp. Miles of it. That cypress grove was so thick and beautiful thirty years ago you couldn't even see through it."

I was shocked. A freshwater forest turned to salt marsh in a single human generation? "What happened to it?" I asked.

Wendy drove a little farther, stopped at a drawbridge. We stepped out and stared at a waterway unlike any of the others I'd seen. Instead of the sinuous curves of the bayous and the snaking labyrinth of the marshes, this huge channel cut a brutally straight line north and south as far as I could see.

"Meet the Houma Nav," said Wendy. The Houma Navigation Canal, finished in 1962, is a 36.6-mile conduit from the open Gulf of Mexico directly to the city of Houma, about fifty miles southwest of New Orleans and one of the centers of the oil industry. When you drive into Houma, a red-and-white sign on the highway says HALLIBURTON WELCOMES YOU TO HOUMA. As hurricanes have taken an increasing toll on Port Fourchon, the coastal town that used to be the center of the oil industry, several companies, including BP, have moved their bases to Houma. The mossy, oak-filled city center is now surrounded by a ring of new chain motels and fast-food joints.

The Houma Nav gave all the boats that run crews and supplies to and from the offshore rigs a straight shot to the city. But it also gave saltwater a straight shot. "That was the beginning of the end for these communities," Wendy said. Every community in the region has badly flooded in each of the hurricanes of the past few years. Water doesn't come up their bayous very easily; instead, it comes straight up the Houma Nav and then spreads out in sheets to the east and west.

Even in calm weather, the water erodes the marsh banks. "When the Houma Nav was built, it was two hundred and fifty feet wide. Now it's eight hundred," Wendy said. As we stood on the bank, a low, black oil barge churned past us, headed for Houma. Its wake sloshed against the bank. A few more grains of dirt crumbled into the canal.

More than nine thousand miles of canals have been dug through the Louisiana wetlands, all of them widening because of erosion and saltwater intrusion. Some, like the Houma Nav, were made to expedite ships' passage. But most were dug by the petroleum industry in its quest for more. Terrebonne Parish sits atop muck that is six miles deep and rich in oil and natural gas. For decades, the industry has carved its way through the marshes, leaving its legacy of eroding canals. Today, if you look at a Google Earth image of Terrebonne Parish, you will be alarmed. Seemingly superimposed on the natural spaghetti of the marshes is a grid of neat lines and right angles, slicing the marsh into rectangles like a sort of giant green precut sheet cake.

And that sheet cake is crumbling. The wetlands of Louisiana are disappearing at a terrifying rate. Not disappearing as in being turned into farmland or housing developments. Not disappearing like the rainforest is disappearing. Disappearing as in oozing into the waves and vanishing forever. Disappearing like a sandcastle disappears into the rising tide. Those wetlands are the birthing centers and kindergartens of the ocean, the places where the next generation of marine life gets its start.

The revelation of what was happening to her beloved wetlands changed Wendy's life. She learned to navigate the labyrinth of backwaters by boat ("GPS set me free!") and began leading eco-tours of the wetlands. She rents out a camp to visiting fishermen and guides fishing trips, too, which are actually clandestine eco-tours. "There's always an ecology angle," she admitted. "I can't help it. When everyone leaves my boat, they know at least one thing they didn't know before." She started a blog called Bayou Woman, wrote a children's book about the disappearing wetlands, and became a fierce advocate for their preservation, speaking to any group that would listen. Then she watched Hurricanes Katrina, Rita, and Gustav wreck her home in succession. Then she watched her husband get diagnosed with early-onset Alzheimer's disease. The Coast Guard wouldn't renew his pilot's license, so he lost his job. Now she was watching oil from the *Deepwater Horizon* seep toward her marshes. And along with it, she was watching her business collapse. "My phone hasn't rung since the day that rig exploded." Who wants an eco-tour of America's greatest environmental catastrophe? I had hoped to go out with Wendy in her boat, but she had pulled it out of the water for lack of business.

"I'm wondering if this is it," she'd confessed over lunch. "Wetland Tours may just fold. Financially, I just can't keep it up. And I may have to sell my camp, because if people can't go fishing, they're not gonna rent it. I'm wondering how many other people are in the same boat. Do I get the jump on them and put my camp up for sale now? Or do I wait another year? Meanwhile, I have to figure out what I'm gonna do. Where can I work? Do I drive to Houma every day? One question I get asked everywhere

I go is 'Why don't you just leave?' People in big cities don't understand. They don't have the connections with where they live
like people who live in a working wetland do. They don't mean
to be offensive with that question, but I find it very offensive. I
just look at them and say, 'Where you from? How long you been
there? You love it? Why don't you just leave?'"

Chapter 3

HOW GOOD IT WAS

THE MISSISSIPPI RIVER is relentless. From its fragile beginnings in the springs of Lake Itasca, Minnesota, all it wants is to get to the sea. Throw any obstacle in its path—a mountain, a dam, a levee—and it will soon slide along or above the object and continue on its single-minded course. That the easiest sea to reach turned out to be the Gulf of Mexico, 2,300 winding miles south, has had a profound impact on America.

Hemmed in by the Rocky Mountains to the west and the Appalachians to the east, the Mississippi drains the water from all or part of thirty-one states—40 percent of America's land—past New Orleans and out into the Gulf of Mexico. Raindrops from Montana and New York State converge in the Gulf. The Mississippi dwarfs other American rivers, with more than twice the drainage area and total discharge of any competitor. But size is not its only distinction. The Mississippi has the honor of draining a very special area: the heartland.

The Midwest is America's breadbasket—not to mention its corn basket, soybean basket, and beef basket. It is a famously fertile place, with all those cattle and cornfields floating atop hundreds of feet of black soil—the real black gold. That black soil was once Canadian rock. Two million years ago, a series of ice ages began, and waves of glaciers marched down Canada, then retreated, then returned in cycles as temperatures bounced up and down. As these walls of ice pushed south, they acted like massive ice scrapers, shaving off most of Canada's dirt, and a good bit of its rock, in fine flakes and pushing it south to the United States in ridges. As the climate warmed and dried, the wind blew these ridges of dust south and west, where they filled the low-lying area of the American plains in fine, mineral-rich sediment. (This is why you don't hit any rocks when you plow the prairie—all the soil there was blown in.) The grasses of the prairie thrived in this fine soil, sinking their roots deep to extract the minerals, drawing carbon dioxide out of the air to build their leaves and roots, and laying down this organic material each winter as they died. Add a few hundred thousand years of buffalo poop as fertilizer, and the result was the richest soil on Earth.

For the past ten thousand years, the Mississippi has been transferring that wealth from the plains of Nebraska and Iowa to southern Louisiana and the Gulf of Mexico. When given its freedom, the Mississippi does not stay in one place. If you had a videotape of the river filmed from space over that time period and played the video on fast-forward, you'd see the river writhing around its valley like an out-of-control fire hose, liquidating its banks, carrying the soil downstream.

At the end of the line, the river delta, you'd see the hose's mouth thrashing back and forth in a spastic arc, emptying its muddy contents into the Gulf of Mexico at different places. You'd also see innumerable brown leaks springing from the hose along its last three hundred miles, soaking the land around it in wet sediment.

That's what you'd see for the first 99 percent of the video. In the closing moments, things would suddenly change. The river would stop thrashing about. Its mouth would fix in place below New Orleans. And all the leaks would be plugged, so that suddenly the land around its last length stayed dry, and all of its muddy contents emptied deep into the Gulf.

But we're getting ahead of ourselves. The immobilizing of the Mississippi in the past hundred years will be a major part of our story, but to understand its consequences, first we need to understand how the system worked for millions of years before that.

The Mississippi is the latest in a long line of noble rivers that have drained the central part of North America. Since South America and North America drifted apart during the Jurassic era, 165 million years ago, opening up the Gulf of Mexico in between, this family of rivers has been depositing its contents into the Gulf. That has helped make the Gulf one of the richest bodies of water on Earth.

It all comes down to algae. Most plant life is found not on land but in the sea, in the form of phytoplankton, single-celled plants such as green algae, cyanobacteria (which used to be called blue-green algae until somebody decided they were closer to bacteria), and a few other organisms. Like their land cousins, phytoplankton create their own food through photosynthesis, using the sun's energy to help them "eat" the carbon from carbon dioxide (dissolved in the sea) and combine it with hydrogen (from good ol' H_2O) to make carbohydrates—sugars and starches. These microscopic plants are responsible for half of the Earth's photosynthesis, half of the basic food supply. They form the marine meadows on which tiny animals graze, beginning the food web that culminates with top predators like dolphins, tuna, and us.

Phytoplankton require the same things as terrestrial plants: light energy for photosynthesis, plus carbon, water, and certain nutrients to make the chemical reactions work, especially nitrogen and phosphorus—the same nutrients we provide our crops in fertilizer. When phytoplankton get all these ingredients, they breed like crazy. A single alga will reproduce once per day, engendering one hundred million descendants in a month. The result is an algae "bloom" as the surface turns into a green pasture.

Some of the nutrients that phytoplankton require tend to sink. In deep water, they'll go all the way to the bottom and be lost, which is why much of the open ocean isn't terribly rich in algae or primary food production. There's just not much "stuff" in the water.

There is, however, a lot of stuff along the coasts. As the rivers course through the land on their way to the sea, they carve nutrients from the earth and deliver them to the surface of the sea, triggering a phytoplankton feeding frenzy. The definition of an estuary is a place where a river meets the sea, and all estuaries are wonderfully rich in life, but the Mississippi River Delta is one of the greenest pastures on Earth. On its single-minded journey from Minnesota to the sea, "Ol' Muddy" scours ultra-fertile farmland and delivers extraordinary loads of nutrients to the Louisiana coast. The Mississippi carries about 145 million tons of dirt to the Gulf every year. Before it was sutured by the present count of twenty-nine locks and dams, which slow down water flow and allow sediment to settle out in reservoirs, it carried around 400 million tons.

It's hard to overstate what an incredible bolus of land this is. For context, the St. Lawrence, Canada's great river, discharges about half the volume of water the Mississippi does, but just 1.5

million tons of sediment, 1 percent of that carried by the Mississippi. Why the difference? Partly because the St. Lawrence drains the rocky Northeast, which doesn't erode as easily as the soft-grained prairies, but primarily because the St. Lawrence gets most of its water from the Great Lakes, nature's premier sediment traps. By the time water exits Lake Ontario, the final stop on the Great Lakes tour, and enters the St. Lawrence, most of its sediment has been left behind at the bottom of the various lakes. In contrast, the Mississippi drains a landscape not blessed with many significant lakes. That, combined with its tremendous power, explains why it pumps out more than fifteen times as much sediment as its nearest competitor in the Lower 48, the Eel River, in Northern California.

That's a big pile of dirt. The actual bedrock of the North American continent dips below sea level before the Gulf Coast is reached. It slopes gradually into the Gulf, extending out for miles to form the continental shelf, before suddenly ending in an underwater cliff. For millennia, the great conveyor belt of the Mississippi and its ancestors has been piling sediment onto this slope. As the sediment pile builds up near the surface, the rest pours over the top of it, filling in the next bit of the slope, continuing farther and farther out. Today, with the Mississippi levee system tightly in place, all that dirt pours right off the edge of the continental shelf, where it is slowly filling the giant, mile-deep hole of the Gulf. But before the twentieth century, when the end of the hose was still leaky and spastic, almost all the dirt came out in a big, spreading fan at the edge of the continent. That's how the delta (any delta, for that matter) was formed. As the dirt at the mouth of the Mississippi built up, creating an obstruction, the mouth of the hose eventually moved, always looking for the easiest path to the Gulf. The mouth of the Mississippi jumped every thousand years or so, fanning across southern Louisiana like a man watering his lawn, forming an overlapping series of deltaic lobes. The Chandeleur Islands, the first land to be hit by the oil spill, are the remnants of one such lobe. Grand Isle and Louisiana's other barrier islands, whose beaches were damaged worst of all, are another.

If you look at a road map of the Gulf Coast, you'll see a fairly straight line of interstate that connects Florida to Houston, traveling through Alabama, Mississippi, and Louisiana. Interstate 10 forms this line for the entire trip except for the hundred miles from Slidell to Baton Rouge, Louisiana, where Interstate 12 bridges the gap. (I-10 dips down through New Orleans.) In Louisiana, that line marks the edge of anything that could be called solid ground. Almost everything south of the line is fill, deposited by the Mississippi and other rivers, and most of it is barely above sea level. In just the past seven thousand years, this fill has extended the coast as many as fifty miles into the Gulf.

And it is a very particular type of coast. As it rolled into the flat delta, Ol' Muddy distributed its waters, especially during floods, into the hundreds of small distributaries wending through the landscape, sometimes for hundreds of miles, before eventually finding their way to the Gulf. These are the smaller bayous of southern Louisiana. (Some of the larger bayous, such as Lafourche and Teche, were the river's main channel thousands of years ago.) During floods, as the muddy water rose over the banks of the Mississippi and its distributaries and spread across the landscape, it slowed, dropping most of its sediment. The net effect was that a fresh inch of dirt was added to all the lands of the Mississippi River Delta in a typical year, like a fresh coating of topsoil.

And waiting to catch that dirt were the marsh grasses. Marsh grasses thrive in places too soggy for trees to grow. Steadily supplied by nutrients from the flooding rivers and bayous, they grow up through them, constantly "climbing," which keeps them ahead of the natural subsidence of the marsh mud. Their dense roots infiltrate every centimeter of the marsh soil and hold it tightly together. They give the marsh a strangely soft permanence. They also give it a kind of sentience. This living, trillion-tentacled entity eagerly grabs particles of sediment and quickly incorporates them into its body, acting like a gigantic carbon filter. By the time water enters the open Gulf, it has left most of its fertility in the marsh.

Which is exactly where you want it. The shallow, brackish, nutrient-thickened, sun-baked water of this southern marsh is an ideal phytoplankton incubator. In addition to this all-you-can-eat salad bar, the marsh provides block after block of public housing, because what many of the sea's small invertebrates need, besides food, is shelter. Juvenile shrimp, for example, live in the shallow edges of the estuaries, hiding out amid the bases of the marsh grasses and nibbling on phytoplankton. What matters for them is the amount of *edge* habitat, where sea and bank meet. The watery capillaries snaking through the marsh grass can support a lot of shrimp, which is why the Mississippi River Delta is an unmatched shrimp maker. Juvenile crabs, snails, and small fish also live in the submerged grasses.

They, in turn, draw larger fish such as redfish, the darlings of Paul Prudhomme and many other Cajun chefs. Sometimes you'll see a reed wriggle as a redfish brushes against it, stalking shrimp, and then see an explosion as the redfish shoots after the prey. Redfish feast in the muddy reeds with their tails sticking out of the water, wallowing like pigs at a trough.

Overall, 97 percent of the commercial fish species in the Gulf depend on these wetlands for their survival. If they don't live, eat, or breed in the marshes, they do so in the submerged areas between the marshes—the oyster reefs and seagrass meadows. Seagrasses are land plants adapted to life underwater, but like their land cousins, they still need light and soil for their roots. To catch the light, they must live close to the surface, so they fare best in the aprons of land just offshore. There, in the well-lit shallows, they form verdant undersea savannas that attract all the grazers of the sea. One acre of seagrass meadow can generate ten tons of leafy food per year, supporting forty thousand fish and fifty million invertebrates. That's a lot of protein.

Seagrasses are easily torn up by wave action from storms, but they have an ancient ally in the oyster. By forming reefs that rise to the surface just off the coast of islands and marshes, oysters create living breakwaters that protect seagrass. And by filtering plankton out of the water, oysters keep it clear so that light can penetrate and reach the seagrass. Part of the goal of the Nature Conservancy's Alabama oyster-restoration project was to create thirty acres of seagrass meadows behind the mile and a half of oyster reef. The intricate labyrinth of spaces in an oyster reef also makes superb housing for the sea's smallest denizens, drawing all sorts of game fish, from Spanish mackerel to speckled trout. This abundance is why ecologists call oysters "ecosystem engineers."

That's just a few tiny strands of the intricate food web spun out in the marshes. Some of those strands stay beneath the surface, but others rise into the air. Birds find everything they need in the marshes: great nest-building material, good cover, and an abundance of food, both in and out of the water. Southern Louisiana contains 40 percent of all the coastal wetlands found in the continental United States, which helps to explain why so many waterfowl call it home. Roseate spoonbills scoop up shrimp in the shallows. White pelicans roost in the cordgrass.

Egrets and herons love to fish from oyster reefs. One fifth of all the ducks in America overwinter in the Louisiana wetlands.

All together, an astonishing 353 species of birds make their homes, or at least seasonal camps, in these marshes. There's more to it than just size and productivity. The Gulf wetlands just happen to fall halfway between the temperate forests of North America and the rainforests of South and Central America, where many of our birds spend their winter. The majority of these birds take the most direct route, straight across the Gulf of Mexico, a good six hundred miles of open water, no stopping. In fall, these wetlands serve as the "Last Gas for 200 Miles" service area. There, the birds rest and refuel before continuing their journey. In spring, sometimes exhausted birds crossing the Gulf rain out of the sky onto the barrier islands and the delta marshes. Without the Mississippi River Delta, this great "migratory flyway," as it's called, would simply not be possible, and America's birdlife would be significantly poorer.

The Gulf Coast is one of those magical places on the planet where life burns a little brighter. A perfect storm of natural conditions has come together to make it incredibly hospitable to so many creatures. Large mammals, however, especially awkward two-legged ones, were not historically on that list. Sure, the coasts were brimming with seafood of every size, shape, and flavor. But they were also short on terra firma and long on mosquitoes. There were few spots where people could throw together some dwellings and settle down, and even those tended to get flooded almost every year.

Beginning about ten thousand years ago, groups of nomadic Indians established a pattern of seasonal life in the wetlands, hunting and fishing during low waters, then escaping to high ground before the floods came. Huge white oyster shell middens on the barrier islands, as well as snail shell middens in the bayous and marshes, attest to the great bounty they took from the region. On land that had some solidity to it, like the Mobile River Delta, some spectacular Native American civilizations arose, but nobody tried to make a go of it in the lowlands.

Until, of course, the Cajuns, who famously were given no choice. The French settled Louisiana in the early 1700s, wisely occupying only the highest natural levees along the river. The rest of the area was a bit sketchy. Sure, the farmland was as good as that in the Midwest—hell, it *was* the farmland from the Midwest— but it had this nasty habit of spending a good portion of its year underwater.

That was just fine with the Cajuns, the first of whom arrived in New Orleans in 1765, back when they were still called Acadians. The Acadians were French Catholics who had settled in the Canadian Maritime Provinces in the previous century to escape persecution in Europe. In the Maritimes they farmed and developed their fishing and trapping skills, which served them well when the persecution caught up with them. When the British took over the Maritimes during the French and Indian War, they expelled the Acadians, sending them to anyone who would take them (and killing quite a few, by way of disease and starvation, in the process). The luckiest Acadians found other sympathetic French Catholics in Louisiana, and eventually four thousand Acadians found their way to the state. Today about a million people call themselves Cajun.

Some Cajuns became farmers in the upper part of Louisiana, depending on the fast-expanding levee system to keep the waters out of their fields. Others saw how good it was in the wetlands and adapted to a way of life hugely dependent on the waters. In the upper reaches of the swamps and marshes, that meant gators and uncountable crawfish. In the lower, brackish marshes, there were oysters and crabs and redfish and shrimp. There they lived, mostly keeping to themselves, and there they might have stayed in relative obscurity, enjoying their economically poor but ecologically and culturally rich bayous, except that in the 1930s, the world discovered that those bayous were floating atop a black gold mine.

Chapter 4

THE BLACKEST SAUCE

M OST PEOPLE BELIEVE it was a horrible coincidence
that the *Deepwater Horizon* oil spill happened so close to
America's most bountiful fishing grounds, but the same factors
that make the northern Gulf of Mexico so rich in life also make
it rich in oil. For the past 165 million years, that great heat lamp,
the southern sun, warmed the broth in the big soup kettle of the
Gulf, and the Mississippi's ancestors poured ingredients into the
pot, cooking up the world's largest batch of algae gumbo. Some
of that algae got eaten by krill or other tiny animals and passed
around the food web, but a lot died and settled to the bottom of
the Gulf along with the sand and other nutrients being pumped
in by the rivers.

The Gulf of Mexico is shaped like a giant's swimming pool,
with a low submerged shelf around its curving edge that then
drops off a cliff into the depths. On the north edge, a steep,
muddy slope plunges from the shallow end to the deep end. That
slope was created by the quadrillions of tons of sediment dumped
down the side of the basin by the Mississippi and its forerunners.
When it blew up, the *Deepwater Horizon* was operating on a well

about halfway down this slope, in a submerged gorge known as the Mississippi Canyon. Many of the deepwater rigs in the Gulf of Mexico are clustered on this slope off the coast of Louisiana, because that's where the oil is.

Plants capture the sun's energy through photosynthesis and use it to build carbohydrates (sugars and starches) out of the carbon dioxide in the air and the hydrogen in water. Carbohydrates are tiny batteries that store solar energy. That energy is locked up in plants' bodies, whether single-celled algae or towering evergreens. Plants power their lives by metabolizing those carbohydrates, as do animals when they eat the plants. Burning the plants is another way of releasing the energy.

Squeeze those carbohydrates long and hard enough, and the carbon and hydrogen atoms get rearranged into hydrocarbons: coal and petroleum. The solar energy is still there, but now in an exceptionally dense form. One gallon of oil holds as much energy as twenty-five pounds of wood, and unleashing that energy is what has powered our civilization for a century.

The recipe for making hydrocarbons is the ultimate in Slow Food: Simmer several billion pounds of greens in a pressure cooker at approximately two hundred degrees for several million years. This occurs naturally when organic matter is buried by enough sediment that the pressure from all that weight raises the temperature. When this happens in swamps, coal is formed. Our coal deposits were created from the immense swampy forests that ruled the planet three hundred million years ago during the aptly named Carboniferous period.

When algae undergoes the same process deep under the sea, however, it gets reduced into the blackest of sauces: oil. All oil deposits are found in places that were once the bottom of highly productive seas. One hundred million years ago, at the height of the Cretaceous period, dinosaurs' finest hour, the lands of the Middle East were at the bottom of one such sea. The Gulf of Mexico was another. Today, with the global climate much cooler than it was during the Cretaceous, seas are hundreds of feet lower. Nearly all the Middle East is high and dry, with its reservoirs of ancient algae buried deep under the sands. The Gulf is still very much around, though smaller than it used to be. What was formerly its shallow edge is now the land of East Texas and Louisiana. There, millions of years ago, waves of phytoplankton bloomed, died, and—instead of decaying, being eaten by bacteria, and returning to the food web—fell to the bottom as "marine snow." There they were covered by tons of sand and other sediment spewing from rivers into the Gulf and slowly cooked into oil.

So the Gulf was flush in the first two conditions needed to make oil: productive seas and a steady supply of sediment to bury the algae and keep it from being recycled. But even that isn't enough to make a great oil resource. Being lighter than rock, oil droplets slowly "migrate" toward the surface through any microscopic gap they can find, forced by the intense pressure miles underground. If they reach the surface, they evaporate, but if they encounter layers of particularly porous rock, they can be trapped in those pores. The best rock for trapping oil is sandstone. Sand, given enough time and pressure, turns into porous sandstone, which will suck up oil like a sponge. About twenty million years ago, sand from the Appalachian Mountains began eroding and pouring into the Gulf of Mexico, where it formed an ideal oil-absorbing layer of sandstone. Those "pay sands," as the lingo goes, have been the quarry of the oil industry for a century. Oil fields are not underground pools. They are layers of oily rock. But they are under such intense pressure that if tapped, the petroleum will shoot out of the rock and to the surface as oil and natural gas.

The best petroleum reservoirs owe their existence to salt. Over millions of years, as global temperatures have shifted, seas have expanded and contracted, leaving sheets of evaporated salt behind, like gargantuan versions of Utah's Bonneville Salt Flats. For millions of years, the Gulf of Mexico acted like a massive salt pond. This expansion and contraction happened so many times, on such a grand scale, that the Gulf's base layer of salt, buried beneath the other layers of bedrock, can be miles thick. But salt doesn't act like rock. Under pressure, it turns fluid, flowing like a glacier, squeezed toward the surface where the pressure is less. As it flows, it leaves behind cavities that slowly fill with whatever rock is above them. In the Gulf, this rock is often oil-bearing sandstone. So instead of a relatively thin, flat layer of oil-rich pay sands, you get a bowl-shaped "trap" filled with them. These traps are where you find the great oil fields. BP's Macondo well lies in such a cavity.

The first oil tapped onshore in Texas, Louisiana, and else-where on the Gulf Coast was found in traps nestled above the salt sheet. Oilmen learned that once their drill bits hit salt, the well was tapped out. And tap they did, peaking in the 1970s. That was the oil boom. By the 1980s, most onshore wells throughout the Gulf Coast had been sucked dry. That was the oil bust, and East Texas and Louisiana became pretty grim places.

The only bright spot in the domestic oil picture in those days was offshore drilling. Petroleum pays no attention to something as ephemeral as the shoreline. It is buried under miles of mud. Whether or not that mud is topped by a few feet of water is mean-ingless, except that it has a profound bearing on our ability to access it.

The offshore game began in 1896, when the first subsea well was drilled in California's Santa Barbara Channel. That well was attached to piers extending from shore. For the next fifty years, all oil wells remained either onshore or just a few miles offshore in shallow water. Then, in 1947, BP established a rig eighteen miles off the coast of Louisiana's Vermilion Parish, in about twenty feet of water, making it the first corporation to drill out of sight of land. Through the 1950s, oil companies began converting the inshore drilling barges that had been operating in the Louisiana marshes to "submersible" mobile drilling platforms. These floated on pontoons for transport but were too unstable to drill while floating (as were the ships of the day). Instead, when they reached their destination, the pontoons would be flooded and sunk until they rested on the sea bottom. The drill deck was built about a hundred feet above the pontoons—and that was the depth limit of offshore drilling.

Then, in 1961, a serendipitous goof: Shell Oil's submersible *Blue Water Rig No. 1* turned out to be too heavy for its pontoons, which completely submerged when the rig was afloat. In this "semisubmersible" position, with the pontoons acting like massive ballast tanks, the rig turned out to be incredibly stable. The first intentional semisubmersible was built in 1963, and suddenly oil fields lying beneath hundreds of feet of water were in play—up to about 600 feet in the 1960s, 1,000 feet in the 1970s, and 1,500 feet in the 1980s.

Offshore technology also put into play new oil reserves off the Atlantic and Pacific coasts, but a spill in the Santa Barbara Channel in 1969, which sent four million gallons of oil onto California beaches and killed thousands of birds and other marine life, galvanized intense environmental opposition on both coasts. Not so on the Gulf Coast, where oil money was often the only decent source of jobs and revenue. The environmental movement was "afraid to challenge [the industry] because of local politics," according to Kierán Suckling, founder of the Center for Biological Diversity. "Or it was unwilling to challenge because it has written off the Gulf as America's dumping ground." A kind of horse trade took place. You give us the Atlantic and Pacific, the environmental groups signaled the industry, and we'll give you the Gulf. A 1981 moratorium banned drilling in federal waters of the United States, except for two key areas: the coast of Alaska and the western half of the Gulf of Mexico.

By the end of the 1980s, all the easily obtained "elephants"—the huge oil reservoirs—above the salt sheet had been pumped, and oil experts began to refer to the Gulf of Mexico as the "Dead Sea." But even as jobs dried up and a general gloom settled on the "Oil Coast," geologists were tapping a mental gusher: They learned that the salt sheet was often a false bottom hiding major treasure.

Seismologists had long been "peering" through bedrock by setting off explosions and reading the echoes that came back through the layers of rock, listening for the telltale thrum of oil reservoirs, but salt, which refracts the sound waves strangely, had always stymied them. Not until the late 1980s did the technology and science become sophisticated enough to glimpse what lay beneath the salt. And what they glimpsed was a complete surprise.

As the base layer of salt beneath the Gulf of Mexico's bedrock flowed like a glacier, it formed complex shapes. If you look at a cross-section of the rock beneath the Gulf, you see the typical layer cake of different rocks from different eras, with crazy veins of salt flowing through it, spurting toward the surface in columns (yes, pillars of salt—though, in this case, pillars eight miles high), then spreading out again into new sheets. Instead of simply marking the bottom, the salt was like the icing in a layer cake—drill through a layer of it and you hit a whole new layer of cake.

And that cake was full of oil. There may be 40 billion barrels of oil lying underneath the deep Gulf. There may be more. Worldwide, there are more than a *trillion* barrels of oil reserves— more oil in the ocean depths than Peak Oilers ever dreamed. In a few years, half of the world's oil will come from offshore wells, most of it from places with far less regulation and control than the United States.

Yet back in the 1980s most of that oil remained unobtainable; it was too deep in the Gulf. The deepwater era began in earnest on December 6, 1989, when Shell woke the moribund Gulf of Mexico oil industry by announcing that it had struck an elephant—at the unthinkable depth of almost three thousand feet. Nobody at the time, not even Shell, had the technology to extract that oil, but the need was clear. Shallow-water production was flatlining at about 280 million barrels per year, and would be declining; U.S. consumption was surging (today we consume about 6 billion barrels per year), and the first Gulf War was about to make many international supplies unreliable.

The first successful sub-salt well was punched through nearly four thousand feet of salt in 1994, and it marked a rebirth for the Gulf Coast oil industry. That rebirth might have stayed modest, given that most of the newly discovered oil lay mingled with salt formations deep under the sea, except that technology kept improving. Exploration ships began towing garlands of sensors for miles behind them, listening to the air gun echoes from the bottom with increasingly acute precision. And drilling platforms kept getting more massive and more complicated—to the point that they outpaced regulators' ability to understand them and make appropriate safety rules.

Still, the huge costs of deepwater drilling made it uneconomic at early-1990s oil prices, which was why Bill Clinton signed the Deepwater Royalty Relief Act in 1995, waiving federal royalties (at the time, 12.5 percent) for deepwater finds as a way to sweeten the pie and ensure energy security. Meanwhile, the Minerals Management Service, which was ostensibly supposed to police the industry, became its accomplice, rubber-stamping almost all drilling permits.

The gold rush was on. Every major player scrambled to get in on the deepwater game, applying for thousands of leases in just a few years.

In 1998, shallow-water production began its inexorable decline, just as the technology to drill in deepwater matured. By 2002, deepwater wells (one thousand to five thousand feet beneath the surface) produced more oil than shallow-water wells. The first ultra-deepwater production (more than five thousand feet beneath the surface) began in 2004. Today it, too, produces more oil than shallow-water fields, and it will soon surpass deepwater wells, though overall offshore production is about what it was a decade ago. The last elephants lurk beneath ten thousand feet of water and five miles of salt and rock. Their home is the last frontier. But it's an expensive frontier. Average "finding costs"—what it takes to prospect for new oil fields and develop the wells (which is what the *Deepwater Horizon* was doing)—are $5 per barrel in the Middle East and more than $63 per barrel in U.S. offshore waters, the highest price in the world. No wonder we became addicted to foreign oil. "Lifting costs"— for the actual mechanics of pumping—add another $10 or so per barrel.

When a barrel of oil sells for less than $75, deepwater exploration doesn't pay, much less ultra-deep. From 1999 until 2004, as oil prices remained historically low, there was little deepwater drilling in the Gulf. Then, prices skyrocketed. The technology was in place, the elephants had been spotted, the country was desperate, and suddenly it was all worthwhile. Oil companies began drooling over the deep plays in the Gulf, as well as those off our other coasts. In March 2008, the price of crude soared past $100 per barrel, then hit an all-time high of $137 four months later. By early 2010, with chants of "Drill, baby, drill" echoing in his brain, Barack Obama signaled his willingness to allow new drilling off U.S. coasts. Congress let the 1981 moratorium lapse, and the stage was set for another black gold rush off western Florida, Virginia, and elsewhere.

In the front lines of that rush were two corporations made infamous by the *Deepwater Horizon*: Transocean and BP. Transocean, the megalithic offshore drilling contractor that owns the *Deepwater Horizon* and many of its kin, likes to use the promotional line "We're never out of our depth." Indeed, Transocean is easily the biggest of the few players in the deepwater drilling game. It owns nearly half of the world's supply of deepwater and ultra-deepwater rigs and more than 130 offshore platforms in all. It can do things no other company can. Transocean is based in Switzerland, but the only thing Swiss about it is its tax burden (twelve of its eighteen thousand employees work in Switzerland); its DNA is pure Houston. And the massive platforms it builds may well be the Parthenons of our time— soaring high-tech temples to the god of the modern world. They incinerate a few million gallons of diesel per year in their multiple, 3,500-horsepower generators, which power the drills, the cranes, the mud pumps, the thrusters that keep the rigs in place, the GPS systems that tell the thrusters what to do, the radar and sonar, the remote submersibles, the living quarters for the hundred-plus crew members, the galleys, the lights and TVs and phones and computers and everything else needed to keep everyone alive and everything functioning in the middle of the open Gulf.

Transocean doesn't sell oil. It doesn't buy leases. It accesses oil, far under the sea, and pumps it for whatever company has hired it to do so. Its clients are a who's who of Big Oil, because nobody else has a deepwater fleet like Transocean's. BP, ExxonMobil, Shell, Chevron, and a few companies you've never heard of all rent Transocean rigs for their deepwater work, and pay Transocean employees to do the work. When the *Deepwater Horizon* exploded, only a handful of the 126 men on the rig were in BP's employ. Most of the rest worked for Transocean. The company's Web site is www.deepwater.com—which once must have seemed like a clever idea.

Despite its dominance in the deepwater field, by 2010 Transocean was beginning to show some cracks. In the years since a 2007 merger with its closest rival, GlobalSantaFe Corporation, Transocean had expanded its ownership of deepwater rigs in the Gulf from 33 to 42 percent, but at the same time, its share of safety incidents serious enough to warrant federal investigation had increased from 33 to 73 percent. Many industry observers believed its level of performance had slid since the merger. In 2009, its top executives lost their bonuses because of the deaths of four rig workers.

About 12 percent of Transocean's earnings come from BP alone, which has embraced the cavalier deepwater game more wholeheartedly than any other oil corporation. In 2009, rigs in BP's hire pumped 182 million barrels of crude from the Gulf, twice as much as its nearest rivals. BP titled its 2009 annual review *Operating at the Energy Frontiers*. As the review makes clear, the Gulf of Mexico was the key frontier: "BP is the leading operator in the Gulf of Mexico. We are the biggest producer, the leading resource holder, and have the largest exploration acreage position . . . With new discoveries, successful start-ups, efficient operations, and a strong portfolio of new projects, we are exceptionally well placed to sustain our success in the deepwater Gulf of Mexico over the long run."

Yet one could argue that BP has been over its head in the Gulf for some time. The once-stodgy British company, which began life in 1908 as the Anglo-Persian Oil Company, carrying out the empire's work in Iran and other Middle Eastern countries, had transformed into a high-tech oil gambler in the late 1990s once it became clear that deepwater was petroleum's future. BP decided to try to beat the Texas oilmen at their own game, setting up operations in Houston and going for broke in the Gulf, especially in deepwater, where many feared to tread. Through the past decade, BP bought up deepwater Gulf leases in what amounted to a flurry of land speculation, investing almost half of its global exploration budget there. But even with the most advanced seismology and the most brilliant engineers, nailing a reservoir deep under earth and sea with a six-mile drinking straw is excruciatingly difficult. The tab for drilling such a hole runs about one hundred million dollars, whether it comes up dry or not—and most do. Many an oil company has gone under in the deep end of the deepwater pool, but BP was willing to take the risk because it knew the rewards were great. Like a poker player with a small stack and nothing to lose, it kept going all-in, hoping it wouldn't get called. It had to. Exxon-Mobile, with its huge stack of resources, could afford to play it slow and safe, but BP didn't have that luxury. It gambled—and, for a while, won, growing into the second-richest player, behind ExxonMobile, by pushing the available technology to the edge out on the rim of the continental abyss. BP's vice president for Gulf production, Kenny Lang, put it this way to the *New York Times* a few years ago: "This is as close as we get to the space age on earth."

Houston, we have a problem.

Chapter 5

"THE UNTHINKABLE
HAS BECOME THINKABLE"

THERE WAS NOTHING remarkable about the Macondo well. The well itself began on the floor of the Gulf of Mexico, about forty-eight miles southeast from the mouth of the Mississippi and 4,992 feet below the surface. From there, it continued more than two and a half miles through the rock of the seabed to a total depth of 18,360 feet below the surface. That sounds staggering to most of us, but in the realm of deepwater drilling, it's ho-hum. When the *Deepwater Horizon* blew up on April 20, Shell's *Perdido* platform, a much newer, fancier rig, was two hundred miles offshore, working in 9,600 feet of water. In 2009, the *Deepwater Horizon* itself had drilled a well to 35,055 feet deep—the current world record.

The *Deepwater Horizon*, however, was not especially fancy, as deepwater rigs go. It was relatively old, having been in commission since 2001, and not nearly as slick as something like *Perdido*, which can suck oil from multiple wells spread across eighty square miles of ocean while simultaneously drilling new holes. The *Deepwater Horizon*, which could work on only one well at a time, was more like a veteran pitcher—solid, dependable, proven, profitable. It worked on all sorts of wells, and it worked a lot. It was even a relief pitcher on the Macondo well, which had been started by the *Marianas*, another semisubmersible, in October 2009. But a month later the *Marianas* was damaged by Hurricane Ida and forced to return to shore for repairs. The *Deepwater Horizon* was brought into the game in February 2010.

The *Deepwater Horizon* was a moneymaker. It had already drilled thirty previous wells for BP. It had found oceans of oil. It never slept. One twelve-hour shift gave way to the next, 24-7, digging the drill bit through another foot of rock under the Gulf of Mexico about every forty seconds, clanking another thirty-foot section of drill pipe onto the end of the three-mile "string" every twenty minutes or so. Its crew had an excellent safety record: seven years without a single serious accident. On the day of the explosion, BP executives had just arrived on the rig to celebrate that record.

Until that day, if those executives had ever lain tossing and turning at night, it wasn't the *Deepwater Horizon* that was keeping them awake. That honor might have gone to BP's *Atlantis*, one of the largest platforms in the world, which was floating three times as far into the Gulf as the *Deepwater Horizon*. It had been pumping oil since October 2007. As one whistleblower recently revealed, 85 percent of the piping and instrument diagrams on the *Atlantis*, and 95 percent of its subsea welding records, have never been approved by engineers. This caused one *Atlantis* manager to warn of "catastrophic operator errors" that could lead to apocalyptic oil spills. The executives' nightmares might also have been filled with visions of BP's monstrous *Thunder Horse* platform, which was built in such haste, with contractors desperately trying to make up time in the schedule, that engineering errors caused the rig to list and nearly sink after a 2005 hurricane, and welding errors caused the underwater pipes meant to carry oil from wells to the rig to be unusable—delaying *Thunder Horse's* in-service date by three years.

Unlike *Thunder Horse*, the *Deepwater Horizon* specialized in exploration wells. It would drill until it hit the pay sands, lining the well with metal casing all the way down, then temporarily seal it with cement plugs, remove its blowout preventer and riser—the flexible pipe that travels from the seafloor to the rig—and move on to the next job, leaving a production platform to move in and pump the oil. That was the plan for the Macondo well, and BP had allotted $96 million and seventy-eight days to the project, though the company hoped to complete it in more like fifty. That's a big spread. Time is always money, but in this case, time was a lot of money. BP was paying Transocean, the rig's owner and operator, $533,000 per day to lease the rig and was spending another $500,000 per day on expenses and contractors. Including its internal costs, BP was blowing through $1.5 million per day on the *Deepwater Horizon*. It had hoped to get the rig started on drilling another well elsewhere in the Gulf in March.

Unfortunately, even the seventy-eight-day allotment turned out to be too rosy a projection. Macondo was a gassy, cantankerous "nightmare well," in the words of Brian Morel, one engineer involved. Another worker called it "the Well from Hell." It was steadily serving up what are known, in classic corporate speak, as "well-control events": surprise "kicks" of pressurized natural gas that escape from pockets of rock and shove the drill bit from below. (Pneumatic shock absorbers on a rig keep a constant pressure on the drill pipe through kicks, wave action, and other events.)

The classic gusher of Texas octogenarians' dreams occurs because oil is trapped beneath the earth under extreme pressure, waiting to be freed from its underground tombs so it can rise roiling like the undead to reanimate our metal and plastic contraptions. When rigs drill into a reservoir, they give the oil a way out, and it will surge to the surface of its own accord unless stopped. You'd think we've all seen enough horror movies to know that we should be very careful before poking around old burial grounds, yet for more than a century we've been tunneling deeper and deeper, like crazed archaeologists, toward the great mass graves of the Mesozoic.

The deeper a reservoir lies, the higher the pressure, the bigger the potential surge. (Picture piling three feet of rock on a water balloon. Now picture piling three *miles* of rock on a water balloon.) Oil itself isn't the primary worry. There are hundreds of types of hydrocarbons in a typical reservoir; the heaviest ones are liquids like oil and diesel, or even semisolids like asphalt; the lightest ones are natural gases like methane and propane. These lighter-than-air gases are what surge up a wellhead first. They are also the most flammable. Controlling the gas is the name of the game.

To do this, companies use drilling mud, a thick solution of water, clay, and extra-heavy compounds such as barium (the stuff you drink before a CAT scan). Drilling mud's first function is to lubricate the diamond-tip drill bit at the front of the drill. Sprayed out of nozzles at the drill tip, it sweeps away the rock cuttings made by the drill bit and flows back up the sides of the well to "mud pits" on the rig, where the cuttings are screened out before the mud gets circulated back into the hole. Having thousands of feet of drilling mud sitting in the well also keeps the well under control. As long as the downward pressure from the weight of all that drilling mud is greater than the upward pressure from the reservoir, the oil and gas can't escape from the rock into the well-bore. The upward force in the Macondo formation was twice that necessary to lift the space shuttle into the sky; the *Deepwater Horizon* had to use enough mud to hold two space shuttles down on the launching pad.

As an emergency backup to the drilling mud, every well is capped with a blowout preventer—a four-story, three-hundred-ton, $25 million stacked series of valves that can be closed by remote control from the rig. It looks like a gargantuan plumbing fixture, which is basically what it is. Some valves, used to temporarily seal the well during construction and testing, are rubber and can be opened and closed. The blind-shear ram, the ultimate fail-safe, is a one-way operation only. It consists of two steel blades, high-powered hydraulic guillotines, that can permanently sever a well by slicing right through the metal pipe when an emergency button is pushed.

The Macondo well was getting close to pay sands when a well-control event occurred on March 8 at 13,305 feet below the surface. The kick of gas was strong enough to lodge the drill bit against the side of the well so thoroughly that it couldn't be freed. (That's the assumption, anyway. It's worth noting that there are no cameras, no remotely operated submersibles, in a drill pipe three miles deep. Everyone is operating blind, inferring what is happening through little more than what goes into the drill pipe, what comes back out the sides, and what the pressure gauges read.) BP was forced to sever the end of the pipe, seal the crippled well with a 2,000-foot-long cement plug, back up to 11,000 feet, and angle off from the original well. Two weeks and $25 million down the drain.

But the real nightmare began after the *Deepwater Horizon* team thought they had finally tamed the well. The rock in the Macondo formation turned out to be particularly crumbly. As the *Deepwater Horizon* team was drilling through it, fissures were always threatening to open and swallow the drilling mud into the earth. This is always a challenge in deep wells, where the intense pressure calls for more drilling mud, which puts more pressure on the sides and bottom of the well and makes it more likely to crack. The *Deepwater Horizon* had already experienced one costly "lost circulation" incident, when a million dollars' worth of drilling mud slithered into a crack in the rock and had to be replaced. Mike Williams, the rig's chief electronics technician, told *60 Minutes'* Scott Pelley that he believed the well had cracked because they were digging too fast, trying to make up for lost time. He recalled a BP manager telling the driller, "Hey, let's bump it up, bump it up"—meaning the rate at which the drill bit was descending. After that loss, the rig team reduced the amount of mud they were using to try to lighten the pressure on the sides of the well.

On April 3 the rig *again* lost all of its drilling mud into the void, this time at a depth of 18,260 feet—after the crew had reached the pay sands. Over the next two days, they plugged the hole with "lost-circulation material" (LCM)—extremely thick fluid mixed with fibrous material that will gum up the space (much like the "junk shot" material that would later be used to try to plug the blowout)—and reloaded new mud, again reducing the amount used to avoid additional cracks. They were now walking a fine line: Much less mud would no longer have enough weight to hold the hydrocarbons out of the wellbore; much more would exert so much pressure that it might blow open the rock or the "fix-a-flat" cement plug. They had originally planned to drill to 20,000 feet, because they believed there might be more hydrocarbons farther down, but if they drilled much deeper, the increasing pressure would require more drilling mud. As a BP engineer stated, the well had "forced our hand." They had already reached productive pay sands, so they decided not to push it. They cautiously drilled another 100 feet, to create a space at the bottom of the well, lower than the pay sands, where debris could accumulate, and called the well complete at 18,360 feet on April 9. Indicators showed that they were into a lot of oil. The Well from Hell might work out after all.

The rig crew spent the next five days cleaning out the well and preparing to decouple and move on to the next job. They needed to insert a cement plug in the bottom of the well that would seal the connection to the pay sands and hold in the oil and gas. Once that was in place, they could set a second, backup cement plug, retrieve their expensive drilling mud by displacing it with seawater, then pull up their riser and blowout preventer and be on their way.

But they encountered further problems. Cement is even denser and heavier than drilling mud. To create a plug, cement must be pumped into the bottom of the well under intense pressure, and BP's engineering team was very concerned that the pressure might open another crack. As John Guide, BP's well team leader, testified, "the biggest risk that was associated with this cementing job was losing circulation. That was the number-one risk . . . based on the fact that we had lost circulation just like that out of the clear blue."

Thus the decision was made to use a high-tech, nitrified foam cement made by Halliburton, the contractor hired by BP to provide the cementing. The foam cement, which resembles gray shaving cream, was lighter than normal well cement and would put less pressure on the wellbore. To further reduce pressure, the team decided to use less cement and to pump it more slowly than usual.

But this introduced its own problems. Less cement would fill less space in the well and have less chance of sealing it completely. What's more, a normal, strong blast of cement will force all drilling mud and any bits of crumbled rock out of the wellbore, yielding a nice, clean, solid cement job, but the low pressure required for the Well from Hell might leave debris that would weaken the integrity of the cement. This would be especially true if the well pipe was not perfectly centered in the hole—which it never is, especially in a crumbly hole like the Macondo well whose sides have been eroding irregularly all along.

Halliburton's engineers were aware of this, which was why their design called for the foam cement to be used in conjunction with twenty-one centralizers—collars with springs that help keep the pipe exactly centered in the well, with about a half inch of space on all sides. This helps ensure that the cement fills the space around the entire pipe, with no weak spots. But the rig had only six centralizers on hand. After consulting with BP's own internal experts, John Guide—the primary decision maker on the job—decided that six would be enough.

Halliburton cement engineer Jesse Gagliano was horrified when he learned this. "I was actually in the office working on it," he later testified, "and when I noticed the problem, I printed it out, and got up to go show BP, and when I came around the corner, I ran into Brett Cocales and Mark Hafle [BP engineers], and I pointed out to them, said, 'Hey, I think we have a potential problem here. There's a potential for flow due to six centralizers.' "

Guide wasn't around when word got to Greg Walz, BP's drilling engineering team leader—the chief designer on the job. After seeing Gagliano's information, Walz sent Guide an e-mail just past midnight on April 16, saying that they needed to "honor the modeling." He even went ahead and took care of it, flying an additional fifteen stabilizers to the *Deepwater Horizon* on April 16, along with an expert to help install them. "I wanted to make sure that we did not have a repeat of the last *Atlantis* job with questionable centralizers going into the hole," Walz explained.

But it turned out that the new centralizers were a different kind than the original six, and Guide worried that they might snag on the blowout preventer while being lowered into the well. In addition, Guide explained by e-mail, "it will take 10 hrs to install them." He decided to skip it.

BP's Brett Cocales e-mailed a colleague that six centralizers might not be sufficient. "But who cares," he added, "it's done, end of story, will probably be fine and we'll get a good cement job. I would rather have to squeeze than get stuck above the [wellhead]. So Guide is right on the risk/reward equation." "Squeezing" means adding another cement layer higher up in the well later on, so Cocales was acknowledging that the cement job might fail.

In fact, there was little reason to believe the cement mixture would work in the first place. Lab tests are always run on foam cement before it is used, and Halliburton's particular formula had failed three separate lab tests that mimicked the way it would be used at Macondo. At least one of these lab tests was shared with BP. (The same type of mixture later failed all nine lab tests conducted by the presidential commission investigating the oil spill. "Halliburton and BP both had results in March showing that a very similar foam slurry design to the one actually pumped at the Macondo well would be unstable, but neither acted upon that data," the commission wrote in its official findings. Halliburton responded to the findings, saying that the mixture it wanted to use had passed preliminary tests, but that BP had changed the formula to a less stable one.)

Why did Halliburton and BP go ahead with a plan to use cement with a high risk of failure? No one knows, but it isn't uncommon for cement jobs to fail at that depth. It doesn't necessarily lead to a disaster, either. Normally, a test would reveal the failure while drilling mud was still in place to keep the gas under control, a "squeeze job" would be added, and everything would continue. Still, Gagliano remained so unnerved about the combination of the foam cement and BP's six-centralizer well design that he sent a report to BP on April 18, stating that the plan could result in "a SEVERE gas flow problem." He was worried enough to send an additional e-mail urging BP to at "least circulate one bottoms up on the well before doing a cement job." This meant making one complete cycle of the drilling mud through the well to remove any cuttings, mud, and pockets of gas, putting less burden on the cement. It would have been an extra safety precaution, though it wasn't part of normal procedure. But BP didn't do a complete circulation before beginning the cement job, either because it didn't want to put additional pressure on the delicate wellbore or because it didn't want to take the time—several additional hours at the slow pump rate being used. Instead, it stuck with its plan. Halliburton grudgingly went ahead and delivered the cement formula, and the rig team set the cement plug in the late-night hours of April 19.

To ensure a good cement seal and to provide an additional layer of protection, cement is pumped through a metal one-way check valve called a "float collar" that sits near the bottom of the well. Like a hinged door, the valve opens in one direction but not the other. A tube in the "doorway" holds the valve open so cement can flow through, but when enough pressure is applied, the tube is shot out of the doorway, to the bottom of the well, and the door swings closed, preventing cement (or anything else) from flowing back up. Normally it takes 400 to 700 pounds per square inch (psi) to shoot the tube out of the doorway and allow the valve to swing closed. But when the rig team tried this on the Macondo well, nothing happened. They couldn't force cement through the float collar at all. Something was obstructing either the float collar or the holes at the bottom of the well through which cement would normally circulate. The rig team kept trying again and again, steadily increasing the pumping pressure to force material to flow. It took nine tries and an extraordinary 3,142 psi to get cement circulating. The rig team interpreted this result to mean that they had now blown out the tube and closed the valves on the float collar, but they may have simply cleared the obstruction, leaving the valves open. The intense pressure may also have damaged the well casing, which is exactly what Bob Kaluza, BP's well site leader, was worried about. "I'm afraid that we've blown something higher up in the casing joint," he muttered to the drill team. Whatever happened, we know that gas flowed up through the cement and the float collar.

The basic initial way to tell whether a cement job has gone well (remember, the rig team is operating blind) is to monitor the "returns" coming back up the sides of the well. For every gallon of cement injected down the drill pipe, a gallon of drilling mud should come back out the well. Obviously, that's far from a comprehensive assessment, so there is an additional test, called a "cement bond log," in which high-tech imaging equipment is lowered down the well. It's the gold standard for revealing weaknesses in cement, but because it can take an additional eighteen hours and add another million dollars of extra costs, it's only used when there are particular concerns about the cement.

If ever there was a cement job screaming out for a cement bond log, it was the nitrified foam in the Macondo well, and in fact, BP had flown a team from the contractor Schlumberger out to the *Deepwater Horizon* specifically to do such a test. Yet BP decided not to do the test after receiving word from the "mud loggers"—the people who monitor the drilling mud flowing out of the hole—that they had received "full returns." One of the enduring mysteries of the blowout is why the mud loggers reported full returns when their monitoring equipment indicated that at least three hundred gallons of material had *not* returned, indicating that a lot of cement had disappeared somewhere. But BP's engineers received word that they had full returns. They decided that the cement job was good, and they flew the Schlumberger team home on the morning of April 20 without having done the cement bond log.

Because cement failures are not uncommon in deepwater conditions, rigs generally do an additional test called a negative-pressure test. Some of the drilling mud is removed to lighten the pressure, an inflatable rubber gasket in the blowout preventer called an "annular preventer" is closed around the drill pipe, temporarily blocking the downward pressure from the mud in the riser, and the pressure is checked. If the cement seals are holding, there should be no negative (i.e., upward) pressure on the pressure gauge in the drill pipe.

According to Jimmy Harrell, Transocean's rig manager, BP actually had no plan to do this multi-hour test—one more sign that it was trading safety for speed. After Harrell refused to go forward without the test, BP relented.

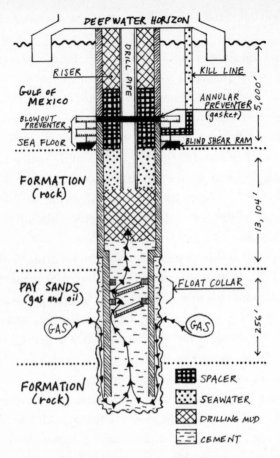

The failed negative-pressure test in the Macondo well (not to scale). The cement plug at the bottom of the well was supposed to keep methane gas in the pay sands from entering the well, but it didn't. Cement may have leaked through a fracture in the bottom of the well. Normally a second, backup cement plug would have been set in the well, but in this case it wasn't. Gas entered the well and was held down by only drilling mud. To do the negative-pressure test, the Deepwater Horizon displaced 8,367 feet of mud with spacer fluid and seawater and closed the annular preventer gasket. The pressure gauge on the drill pipe should have read zero, but it registered 1,400 psi of pressure coming up from below. The kill line should have had the same reading, but because of a leak in the annular preventer, it was clogged with spacer fluid and showed zero pressure. The crew chose to ignore the drill pipe reading. They opened the annular preventer and displaced the rest of the drilling mud, giving the gas an open path to the rig. Illustration by Mary Elder Jacobsen.

The *Deepwater Horizon* team (all of whom worked for Transocean) had done many negative-pressure tests. They knew the protocol. Set a backup three-hundred-foot cement plug above the first, just in case. Let that harden. Then do the test. If everything pans out, then go ahead and replace the valuable drilling mud with seawater. This was how BP had planned to do the procedure as late as April 14. Yet by April 20, the plan had changed. At a midday meeting, when one twelve-hour shift was briefing the next, Bob Kaluza informed the rig team that they wouldn't be doing it that way this time. This time, they were going to replace the mud with seawater *while* doing the negative-pressure test, then set the backup cement plug afterward.

Kaluza himself, who was taking last-minute orders from BP's engineers in Houston, didn't understand the rationale behind the change. "Don't know why," he later admitted. "Maybe trying to save time. At the end of the well sometimes they think about speeding up." By April 20, Day 80 on the job for the *Deepwater Horizon*, the budget was long blown. BP's last estimates were that the project would cost $140 million—$44 million more than the initial budget. There's no evidence of anyone being ordered to speed things up, but the pressure to finish must have been in the back of everyone's mind.

Kaluza was new to the deepwater game. His career had been on land, and this was just his fifth day on the rig. He'd come out, he said, "to learn about deep water." He was about to get an education. Kaluza's predecessor on the rig, who had much more deepwater experience, acknowledged to investigators that he had never, ever heard of such a move during a negative-pressure test.

Neither had any of the Transocean workers at the meeting that day. Dewey Revette, the driller, reacted strongly, making it crystal clear that he thought such an action was dangerous and foolish. Revette argued furiously with Kaluza, and soon Jimmy Harrell joined in on Revette's behalf. No dice. Kaluza said, "This is how it's gonna be," and Harrell disgustedly replied, "Well, I guess that's what we have those pinchers for"—meaning the blind-shear ram, the horizontal guillotines designed to snap shut on the neck of the pipe in case of a total loss of control.

The change in protocol made no sense except as a time-saving move. Instead of waiting hours for the cement plug to set before doing the negative-pressure test, and only beginning to remove the mud if the test had been successful, BP could get started immediately. The decision made a mockery of safety precautions, especially in light of all the concerns about the foam cement. But it sure saved time.

At 1:28 P.M., the *Deepwater Horizon* began pumping mud out of the well and into a tank in the *Damon Bankston*, a supply ship stationed alongside it, a process that went on for nearly four hours.

Late in the afternoon, they began the negative-pressure test. And here BP did something very unusual. The first step in the test is to displace mud in the well by pumping down seawater, but mud and water can't mix, so they must always be separated by a "spacer" fluid. BP happened to have a lot of lost-circulation material—the "fix-a-flat" gunk—left on the rig that it had to dispose of. Environmental regulations say that LCM must be disposed of on land in waste disposal sites—an expensive and time-consuming trip. But there is a loophole. Any material that comes up from the well, including LCM, can be dumped overboard. All BP had to do was send the LCM down the well and it could dispose of its whole disposal problem. It decided to use the LCM for the spacer fluid. The mud experts on the rig said fine, and down the hole it went.

At 4:54 P.M., the rubber annular preventer on the blowout preventer was closed. Things did not go according to plan. The pressure gauge showed 1,400 psi of upward pressure from below. Three times, the crew bled the pressure off through the drill pipe and repeated the test. Each time, the gauge went back to 1,400 psi. Then the crew noticed that more than six hundred gallons of LCM spacer fluid had leaked down through the annular preventer. It was not sealing tightly.

In fact, there was good reason to suspect that the annular preventer was damaged. Back in March, Mike Williams told *60 Minutes*, something had gone wrong during a test. With the rubber annular preventer closed tight around the drill pipe, a rig worker had unknowingly raised the drill pipe, forcing it through the tightened seal. Shortly after that, a worker discovered chunks of rubber in the drilling fluid circulating back to the rig. "He thought it was important enough to gather this double handful of chunks of rubber and bring them into the driller shack," Williams said. "I recall asking the supervisor if this was out of the ordinary. And he says, 'Oh, it's no big deal.' And I thought, 'How can it be not a big deal? There's *chunks* of our seal now missing.'" At best, the annular preventer was worn.

As it happened, the BP executive tour arrived at the drill shack, the control center, as the drill team was puzzling over the leaky annular preventer. Jimmy Harrell, who had been leading the tour, stayed behind to help as the tour moved on. He ordered the hydraulic pressure on the annular preventer increased, pushing it tighter against the drill pipe, and that stopped the leakage. Harrell rejoined the tour.

Bob Kaluza, BP's well site leader, was perplexed by the results of the test and put any decisions on hold until his more experienced counterpart, Don Vidrine, came on duty at 6 P.M. Vidrine was also concerned by the results and questioned Kaluza and Transocean's drill team for an hour. Jason Anderson, the toolpusher (who oversees the drilling floor), and Dewey Revette, the driller, had an explanation for the anomalous drill pipe pressure reading, according to BP's investigation: "According to witness accounts, the toolpusher proposed that the pressure on the drill pipe was caused by a phenomenon referred to as 'annular compression' or 'bladder effect.'" (The idea was that mud in the riser was pushing down from above and affecting the pressure gauge.) "The toolpusher and driller stated that they had previously observed this phenomenon. After discussing this concept, the rig crew and the well site leaders accepted the explanation. The investigation team could find no evidence that this pressure effect exists."

Several observers interpreted this line as BP's trying to throw Transocean's rig crew under the bus, but the presidential oil spill commission also couldn't find any experts who had ever heard of such an effect. This is another mystery of the *Deepwater Horizon* disaster. Faced with a reading that might signal a potential catastrophe—and threaten their own safety—it seems inconceivable that the toolpusher and driller would have casually written it off. Unfortunately, we can't ask them what they were thinking; both men died in the explosion. We can't ask Vidrine, either—he has stayed in his house since the disaster and refused to testify, citing health issues.

Vidrine decided they needed to rerun the negative-pressure test before proceeding. Again the well was sealed, and again the pressure rose to 1,400 psi and stayed there. Something had clearly bypassed the cement plug and was pushing from below, wanting up. Yet that wasn't how the men interpreted it. Not trusting the drill pipe pressure reading, Vidrine and Anderson decided to check the pressure in a second, smaller pipe, called the kill line. Indeed, the kill line gauge showed no pressure. Yet the two pipes were connected to the same area and should have had the same readings. No one is sure why the kill line showed no pressure; it may have been clogged by the leaking LCM spacer fluid—which, after all, was designed to clog small holes.

Instead of playing it safe and questioning the kill line reading, Vidrine decided to accept it as a successful negative-pressure test, ignoring the drill pipe reading. When Jimmy Harrell checked in to see how the test had gone, Vidrine told him that they had had "a good negative test for thirty minutes." At 7:55 P.M., Vidrine made a fateful decision. "Go call the office," he said. "Tell them we're going to displace the well." He was ready to replace the rest of the mud with seawater.

Five minutes later, the annular preventer was reopened and the rig began pumping out the rest of the drilling mud—the only thing now holding the gas down, since the second cement plug hadn't yet been set. At 8:52 P.M., enough mud had been removed that the gas began to surge up the well. At that point, the only thing that could have stopped it was the blowout preventer—which was designed to do just that. The gas was still forty-six minutes away from the blowout preventer, fifty-four minutes away from the rig, and it gave the rig team a few signs that it was on its way. As gas rises from the high-pressure depths to the surface, it expands to 800–1,000 times its original volume. By 9:08 P.M., 1,638 more gallons of fluid had exited the pipe than had been pumped in, because the gas was pushing it out as it rose and expanded. And the pressure in the pipe steadily increased.

Yet nobody noticed. BP chalks this up to "simultaneous end-of-well activities." Some drilling fluids were getting a "sheen test" to determine whether they could be legally dumped overboard. (They were.) The final cement plug, which would replace the blowout preventer as the backup barrier, was being prepared. And the senior management was entertaining the BP executives on the bridge with a rig-simulator video game.

A critical moment came at 9:31 P.M., still seven minutes before the gas had reached the blowout preventer. The pumps on the rig that were pushing seawater into the pipe to displace the remaining mud were shut down to fix a mechanical problem— likely caused by the gas. Yet even with the pumps off, at least 2,500 gallons per minute were gushing out of the well. Amazingly, no one noticed.

At 9:40, water, then mud, exploded out of the pipe like a runaway space shuttle, splattering the drill floor and the rig, surging up through the derrick, raining everywhere. Mud—and, according to some reports, small bits of cement—shot out with such force that it even rained down on the *Damon Bankston* off the side of the rig.

Chris Pleasant, Transocean's subsea supervisor, who was in charge of the blowout preventer, was in his office, signing off on end-of-well paperwork. "Chris, what's that water?" asked a colleague who was sitting next to him, watching a video monitor of the rig floor. "They're probably coming out the hole," Pleasant replied. "I see mud," said the colleague. Pleasant called the drill shack. No one answered. "We got to go!" he said, running toward the rig floor.

In the drill shack, someone, probably Jason Anderson, immediately closed the rubber annular preventer in the blowout preventer. But again it didn't seal properly, and the gas continued surging up the pipe. As Anderson raced to engage the variable bore ram, another cutoff on the blowout preventer, an assistant driller in the drill shack called the chief toolpusher. "We have a situation!" he said. "The well is blown out. We have mud going to the crown."

"Do y'all have it shut in?" the toolpusher asked.

"Jason is shutting it in now," came the reply.

Someone on the bridge radioed the *Damon Bankston* and advised it to stand off five hundred meters.

Jason Anderson called Don Vidrine and told him that they were getting mud back, that he had diverted the flow to the mud-gas separator, and that he was trying to close the annular preventer.

The mud-gas separator is a system designed to remove gas from the drilling fluid before the fluid is recirculated down the well. It is a part of normal operations. The other option would have been to divert the flow straight off the side of the rig, which would have been safer. In fact, Transocean's well-control handbook states, "At any time, if there is a rapid expansion of gas in the riser, the diverter must be closed (if not already) and the flow diverted overboard." Doing so is a serious violation of federal environmental regulations, but appropriate for emergencies. The mud-gas separator can handle only small amounts of gas, and it feeds through the heart of the rig, where the diesel engines are.

At 9:46, the mud stopped gushing. "It just quit," said one worker. "I took a deep breath, thinking that, 'Oh, they got it under control.'" But they hadn't. The mud quit because most of it had all been pushed out of the riser. Now gas came hissing out of the pipe and expanding furiously on the rig floor. Gas alarms across the rig went berserk.

At 9:47, Anderson did indeed manage to activate the variable bore ram on the blowout preventer, temporarily shutting off the well. After the accident, there was wide confusion in the press, and among the public, on this point. The blowout preventer *did* engage—but too late. It had no effect on the gas already above it, but it could have prevented additional oil and gas from spilling out of the well long enough for rig workers to permanently seal the well by engaging the blind-shear ram—if they had gotten the chance. The variable bore ram, never intended to be more than a temporary seal, soon came undone.

At that moment, the rig began to shake and roar as the gas filling the floor was sucked into the diesel engines, which began to whine as they ran out of control. Mike Williams described the moment on *60 Minutes*: "I hear the engines revving. The lights are glowing. I'm hearing the alarms. I mean, they're at a constant state now. It's just, 'Beep, beep, beep, beep, beep.' It doesn't stop. But even that's starting to get drowned out by the sound of the engine increasing in speed. And my lights get so incredibly bright that they physically explode. I'm pushing my way back from the desk when my computer monitor exploded."

At 9:49, the power on the rig died and the *Deepwater Horizon* went dark. The chief toolpusher was reaching for his hard hat so he could run to the drill shack. The assistant driller was scrambling toward the door to the drill floor to help. Others were smelling gas and running for their lives. Mike Williams pushed himself back from his exploded computer monitor and reached for a metal door when the gas filling the rig finally found its spark. An explosion ripped across the *Deepwater Horizon*, blew the metal door off its hinges and took Mike Williams with it into the wall on the opposite side. The rig's crane operator was blown off the derrick to his death.

Ten seconds later, there was a second explosion, and the *Deepwater Horizon* was doomed. Eleven men died in the explosion and fire. But even then, there was hope to contain the well and limit the oil spill. Chris Pleasant, the subsea supervisor, scrambled through the fire and chaos to the bridge, where he decided to initiate the emergency disconnect sequence. This emergency button severs the rig from the well and triggers the blind-shear ram on the blowout preventer. The *Deepwater Horizon* had been forced to do just that seven years earlier, when a storm overpowered its thrusters and blew it too far from its well. The system had worked perfectly. "I'm EDSing!" Pleasant told the rig captain. Amazingly, the captain told him, "Calm down, we're not EDSing." Don Vidrine was standing beside Pleasant and asked, "They got the well shut in?" But Pleasant had only one thing on his mind: "I'm getting off here," he said. Vidrine replied, "Yeah, hit the button." Pleasant punched in the EDS sequence. But nothing happened. Pleasant later testified that the system "had no hydraulics." Even without them, the loss of communication with the rig should have triggered the automatic mode function, firing the blind-shear ram, but it didn't.

The captain gave the order to abandon ship. Survivors were already bailing into lifeboats and jumping over the side in a chaotic scramble. Mike Williams was abandoned on the rig, bleeding and dazed. He jumped ninety feet into the water, which was covered in flaming oil. He swam out of the oil and was pulled to safety by the crew in one of the boats.

Jimmy Harrell made it to a lifeboat and then to the *Damon Bankston*, where two witnesses overheard him speaking by phone with someone in Houston. "Are you fucking happy?" he screamed. "Are you fucking happy? The rig's on fire! I told you this was gonna happen."

In the first days after the accident, BP still had high hopes to seal the well and limit the damage, because the blowout preventer had two backup systems that were supposed to automatically trigger the blind-shear ram. The automatic mode function was supposed to engage anytime communication from the rig was cut off. On the morning of April 22, a robot submersible snipped the cables to the burning rig. But the blind-shear ram didn't budge. Later that same day, a robot pulled a pin between the riser pipe and the blowout preventer, trying to "trick" the blowout preventer into thinking that the rig had drifted too far away and pulled off the riser pipe. The blowout preventer "rocked and settled." But the oil flow continued. The blind-shear ram had probably engaged—but it hadn't managed to stanch the flow. Its blades may well have been damaged by the launchpad-level pounding of the runaway well over the past thirty-three hours. One expert estimated that this would happen after just minutes of exposure to the corrosive force of the sand mixed in with the gas.

After burning for two days, the *Deepwater Horizon* sank, tearing the riser pipe. And 205 million gallons of oil—and twice that much natural gas—flowed into the Gulf over the next eighty days.

We're all much too familiar with the aftermath. The Coast Guard's initial claims that the leaking oil was merely what was stored on the rig. Then the "discovery" that 1,000 barrels per day were leaking. ("A game changer," the Coast Guard called it.) Then BP's denial that 5,000 barrels per day were flowing. Then the poignant absurdity of BP clinging to the 5,000-barrels-per-day estimate while it was capturing around 15,000 barrels per day through a tube—and barely making a dent in the flow.

We're also familiar with BP's tragicomic attempts to plug the well during those days. The top hat. The top kill. The junk shot. The calls to Kevin Costner about his oil-spill centrifuge. The desperate scramble to find boats to contain the surface oil. All of these half-assed solutions made it abundantly clear that no one involved had ever suspected that a blowout preventer could utterly fail and leave them with a runaway well a mile below the ocean surface, so no serious contingency plans in how to deal with such an event had ever been completed.

In the days after the explosion, as its fleet of undersea robots tried one after another last-ditch attempt to close the blind-shear ram, BP stressed the virtual impossibility that the blowout preventer could fail. With so many fail-safes, the uncontrollable blowout was one in a million, bad luck, a perfect storm of errors not likely to be replicated. "The unthinkable has become thinkable," said BP spokesperson Andrew Gowers. It had happened, yet it certainly didn't mean that BP or Transocean had been negligent, or that more government-led oversight and safety precautions, god forbid, might be necessary. It was a freak event, a black swan.

Yet Nansen Saleri—former head of reservoir management for Saudi Aramco, Saudi Arabia's state-owned oil company, and now the world's leading authority on oil-reservoir management—was a little more blunt in his assessment, calling the event "a catastrophic failure of risk management."

I have to agree. No one decision or failure single-handedly caused the explosion of the *Deepwater Horizon*. The failed cement on its own could have been detected and remedied. The float collar could have isolated the hydrocarbons. A second cement plug could have been set before the mud was removed from the riser. The negative-pressure test could have alerted the rig team to the presence of gas in the well. Someone monitoring the pressure gauges as the gas rose could have noticed it and given the crew more time to prepare. And when the gas arrived, it could have been diverted over the side. None of these things on its own was a big deal. But because each was the responsibility of someone different, the failures weren't communicated, so nobody knew that the next step had to take more of the burden.

Ultimately, all of the burden fell on the blowout preventer, and it wasn't up to the task. A *New York Times* examination of the history of blowout preventers showed that failure was quite thinkable all along, if anyone had bothered to think it through. The blind-shear ram is only as good as its hydraulic fluid, which provides the force to close the blades, and studies showed that a single valve on the blowout preventer, which had no backup, could easily leak—the dreaded potential "single-point failure." Even when the rig had full hydraulic power, the blind-shear ram's blades weren't strong enough to slice through the thick steel joints found where two sections of pipe connected—and, at the critical moment, they had about a one-in-ten chance of hitting such a joint. That's exactly what happened off the Louisiana coast in 1997, when a blowout preventer failed to prevent a blowout.

This is one of the reasons why up-to-date rigs in the Gulf carry blowout preventers with two blind-shear rams. All of BP's other leased rigs in the Gulf have dual blind-shear rams, as do the eleven Transocean deepwater rigs built since the *Deepwater Horizon*. (Most of the rigs in the Gulf, however, are older, simpler, shallow-water models carrying just one.) The *Deepwater Horizon* had been such a workhorse that it was years overdue to be taken offline to have its blowout preventer updated. (In fact, later forensics found that maintenance on the unit was so overdue that one control pod on the blowout preventer had a faulty solenoid and the other had a dead battery.) Yet even back in 2001, the year the *Deepwater Horizon* was launched, a government report recommended that all deepwater blowout preventers be outfitted with dual blind-shear rams, because of the number of failures in testing.

Even if they don't land on a joint, some blind-shear rams, which have been in operation for years, are too weak to slice through modern deepwater drill pipe, which is far stronger than older pipe. While blowout preventers almost always pass their standard tests—the *Deepwater Horizon* blowout preventer had been tested the very day of the accident—many analysts suspected, even before April 20, that the intense pressure of the deepwater environment, combined with the overwhelming force of a blown-out well, would be a test of another order. West Engineering Services, an industry safety specialist, found that only three of seven blowout preventers successfully sheared pipe in realistic emergency conditions. The most exhaustive study to date, a Norwegian analysis of fifteen thousand wells drilled between 1980 and 2006, found that blowout preventers had been called into action eleven times. They had managed to seal the well just six.

When the shit hits the fan, blowout preventers seem to save the day about half the time. Industry and government experts have known this for years. Yet they have often pushed for *less* testing, *fewer* precautions. We'll never know whether the rig workers on the *Deepwater Horizon* were aware that the difference between their incident being just one more tragic industrial accident and the biggest oil spill in American history was a coin toss. What we do know is that the coin got tossed. And everybody lost.

Chapter 6

SAILING THE SLICK

S OUTH OF MOBILE Bay, Alabama, the mud of the coast
gave way to the gray-green waters of the Gulf of Mexico.
Stately breakers rolled across our bow. *Dolphin's Waltz*, our
forty-three-foot sailboat, loved it. She'd been built twenty-
seven years ago with oceans in mind. Wide of beam, thick of
hull, with eleven thousand pounds of lead in her keel, she was sick
of putzing around shallow Mobile Bay, where she was docked.
She needed to get out.

We passed within kissing distance of a couple of gas rigs,
their motors shrieking, dodged a pack of shrimp boats searching for oil slicks, their spars deployed like giant grasshoppers,
and made for Dauphin Island Pass and the open Gulf. We were
the only pleasure boat around. A Coast Guard chopper slashed
overhead and a blimp hung in the southern sky like an alternate
moon. A west wind snapped the jib taut. The sun hammered
through a tropical haze. It was ninety-five degrees. A pod of dolphins hustled across the water and hot-dogged across our bow
wave, exploding into the air as they caught it. For being smack in

the middle of America's biggest environmental disaster, it was pretty damn nice.

You might say that July 2010 was an odd time for a pleasure cruise in the Gulf of Mexico. And you'd be right. You might say that a sailboat—slow, bulky, with the upwind quarter of the world off-limits at any given time—is an odd way to do any sort of journalism. Right again. I certainly wasn't going to scoop the *Wall Street Journal* aboard *Dolphin's Waltz*. But that was the point. Let the press hordes stampede past us in their copters and vans, chasing the latest oil sighting. Sailing at five knots, we hoped to travel slowly and quietly enough that we might just sneak up on the soul of this place before it spooked.

Thus we'd set off on a wind-powered tour of a particularly stunning corner of the Gulf. We would visit Petit Bois Island (pronounced "Petty Boy" in Gulf Coast lingo), the most pristine wilderness island in the Gulf and vital habitat for more than 250 species of birds, where there were rumors of cleanup operations gone awry: ATVs run amok in the dunes; workers threatening the eggs in the rookeries. From Petit Bois we would cross Mississippi Sound to see the oyster reefs and seagrass meadows of Grand Bay, taking in as many marine ecosystems in three days as you could hope to do on a sailboat. We would use fossil fuel only when absolutely necessary—which we knew it would be. Motors are automatic on sailboats these days, and the boats are docked in slips like parking spaces. Not even Dennis Conner could sail out of one of those. Getting out of the Mobile Yacht Club involved making several right-angle turns, negotiating a narrow harbor, passing under a bridge, then following a dredged shipping channel out of Mobile Bay. Only then does the water get deep enough for maneuverability. If you're under sail and the wind is blowing from the wrong direction, you're screwed. The world is no longer wind-friendly.

Fortunately, our first day was friendly enough that as soon as we'd cleared the bridge and caught the shipping channel, we were able to kill the motor and raise the sails. Close-hauled to the wind, we heeled over and shot straight out the channel toward the Dauphin Island Pass. In seconds the smell of diesel faded, replaced by the slow oscillation of wind and wave. Free at last.

Not that we were making any kind of statement. Our entire crew had burned piles of carbon just getting to the Mobile Yacht Club. For me, that involved flying into Newark, New Jersey, where I looked down upon a grid of refineries and tanks, then to Houston, same damn thing, then to Mobile. Oil was everywhere and in everything, not just the Gulf.

Mobile Bay was crawling with boats as we sailed out. Two inflatables came shooting out of the back of a Coast Guard cutter. On the western shore of the bay, a petroleum facility's orange methane flare blazed atop a black pillar like something out of Mordor.

Vessels of Opportunity—individual boats hired by BP to patrol for oil—darted across the shipping channel. The program was the biggest gold rush on the coast. Even the smallest boats made $1,600 per day. The shrimp boats we saw were pulling in a few thousand a day, plus fuel. There were about three thousand VOOs, as everyone called them, operating in Alabama, Mississippi, and Louisiana. They came in every size and shape—million-dollar sportfishing behemoths, Boston whalers, even pontoon boats that would have looked more comfortable on an Adirondack lake. I tried not to think about how much gas they were burning in the effort to save us all from oil. All flew the triangular VOO flag, and all seemed to be zipping about with minimal coordination. A mullet skiff whipped by, VOO flag snapping, and a big, dreadlocked dude on the bow saluted us. A sportfishing boat, the *Ragin' Cajun*, cut directly across our bow, its wake crashing against us. Not everybody likes "stickboats" in these parts.

Yet as we passed within twenty yards of one gas rig, a man on the catwalk waved his arms and shouted. I thought maybe he was angry at us for passing so close, but Jimbo Meador, one of our crew, said, "He's saying he wishes he was on this boat and not on that goddamn rig." Jimbo is a Gulf Coast legend, born and raised on the Alabama shore. "When I was growing up, we used to hunt quail by horseback in our backyard," he said. His first job was collecting seagrass and selling it to fish stores. He is one of the best fly fishermen on the Gulf and, because he does it all by kayak and stand-up paddleboard, one of the fittest sixty-eight-year-olds you'll ever see. The water has been his life. He makes a point of swimming in it every day. "If I get too far from saltwater, I start to get nervous," he told me. With his deep tan and wavy gray hair, he looks like a man who had been crystallized out of the waters and sea foam, then strode out of the surf and began throwing a cast net. If anyone had a lot at stake in the health of this place, it was Jimbo.

Our other crew member was Bill Finch. Bill knew Jimbo, knew me, knew the owner of *Dolphin's Waltz*. Bill had pulled this unlikely trip together. He'd heard about BP's minions tromping all over Petit Bois and wanted to check it out. Plus he still wanted to get me out to those islands and oyster reefs in the middle of Grand Bay.

Our skipper, Josh Deupree, was the fleet manager at the Mo-

bile Yacht Club and one of the top sailboat racers on the Gulf
Coast. He'd grown up on the water, living a very typical Gulf
boy's childhood, of which Petit Bois had been a memorable
part of the scenery. "My family used to go out there on weekends," he said. "It was like *Gilligan's Island*. We'd meet up with
other boats. While sailing on the way down, we'd troll for
Spanish mackerel, then put 'em on the barbecue. We'd anchor
up and put the Windsurfer together and fish. We'd catch speckled trout, flounder. It was real nice." Josh had been hesitant to
take *Dolphin's Waltz* out of port for fear of mucking up the hull
and engine with oil, yet his curiosity about what had befallen
Petit Bois won out. Besides, he couldn't resist the lure of a few
days on the water. To Josh, heaven is open water, powerful
winds, and waves frothing over the leeward rail. He was more
than happy to keep the motor off.

In the open Gulf, we continued to slalom through the rigs. If,
like me, you grew up on the East Coast, you may still have the
quaint notion that when you stand on a beach and look out to
sea, you will see nothing but blue horizon. People who live on
the Gulf Coast have no such romantic expectation. More than
four thousand active gas and oil rigs pepper the Gulf. While
Grand Bay and Petit Bois were part of the scenery of Bill's and
Josh's childhoods, the rigs are the scenery of many Gulf Coasters'
lives. They are where you head to catch red snapper, because the
fish cluster beneath the rigs. The *Deepwater Horizon* and its kin
may be the Parthenons of our time, but the majority of rigs are
still more like rinky-dink one-room churches, sticking closer to
shore where they can attach to the seafloor. Many of these have
been abandoned; many others limp along.

A few miles off the coast of Petit Bois, we hit the first

brick-colored slick. It looked like a thin trail of diarrhea running to the southern horizon. Our bow punched through it, it disappeared behind us, and the Gulf was green again. We hit a few more slicks as we approached the island. Sailing has been defined as hours of boredom interrupted by moments of terror. This was hours of beauty broken by moments of disgust.

A line of trees on the horizon. Petit Bois. A typical barrier island: a wandering carpet of sand and dunes that gets piled just high enough on the inland side to support a few marshes and trees. These trees—which had given the island its name, courtesy of early French sailors—seemed mostly dead, a casualty of Hurricane Katrina. Petit Bois is part of Gulf Islands National Seashore. In 1978 it was designated as wilderness, the U.S. Park Service's highest level of protection. Here's Congress's official definition of wilderness: "An area where the Earth and its community of life are untrammeled by man . . . it must generally appear to have been affected primarily by the forces of nature, with the imprint of man's work substantially unnoticeable." Yet as we approached, we could see blue shapes at regular intervals along the beach. Through binoculars, they revealed themselves as tents, each shading an assemblage of coolers, rakes, and plastic chairs. No one was around. Just the beach and the tents. It was like something out of a Beckett play, *Waiting for Godot* with hydrocarbons.

The sun was oozing orangely into the Gulf as we anchored in the lee of the island. The island was deserted, but the lagoons on the lee side were fenced with bright-yellow boom, and anchored offshore was a clot of crew boats, barges, and tenders. The barges were stacked with double-decker, forty-foot-long steel boxes stamped LIVING QUARTERS on the side—shipping containers modified into windowless "flotels." This was where

Hazmat Nation spent its evenings. I wondered how many were squeezed into each tin.

Anchored near us was a massive, three-story sportfishing boat flying a VOO flag. It never moved the entire time we were there. A couple of guys in camo fatigues lolled on the upper deck.

Gulf Coasters know the Vessels of Opportunity program is a boondoggle. The boats' ability to deal with any oil they find is very limited, as explained by one VOO captain who agreed to speak with me anonymously. "If we found anything," he said, "we'd call the shrimp boat that was assigned to us, and they would come, and then we'd boom it off and suit up in Tyvek. We had these aluminum-welded poles that we'd put a plastic bag, like a produce bag, on the end of, and you'd actually scoop the oil up with those bags, and then you'd bag it up in big plastic bags and drop it off. We got as much as we could, but it was almost pointless. We can't really clean that shit up."

With BP footing the bill for the VOO program, no one would really mind the boondoggle—it's a sort of disgrace tax—except the cash was often going to the wrong people. The idea was to employ out-of-work fishermen, but my VOO mole—a sportfishing guide—explained that it hasn't worked that way. "At first it was ridiculous. There was no supervision. Zero. You'd just check in, leave the dock, see ya in twelve hours or whatever. People were going out and fishing all day and collecting their money. Early on, there was no sign of anything within a hundred miles of Mobile Bay. Your assignment was to go patrol and watch for broken pieces of boom or boom that's come unanchored. Allegedly, there were guys who were going out at night and cutting up the boom, giving themselves what they thought was job security. I wouldn't put it past some of those boys."

Despite the fact that his guide business had dried up with the

Deepwater Horizon blowout, it had taken my VOO mole a while to get activated in the program. "There were several people out there not in the fishing business who, when this whole thing first happened, went and formed corporations and got boats entered into the VOO program. I know for a fact one group had nine boats operating out there for a couple of months every single day. They had their friends' kids operating the boats. And you'd call BP and ask, 'When am I gonna get activated,' and the response would be, 'Well, we've got too many people. We'll call you as need arises.' A good friend of mine, a young kid, got involved in this at the onset. Bless his heart, he needed the money bad, but he was out there for two months in a twelve-foot johnboat. *Two months!* In a twelve-foot boat! You can't blame him for doing that. But how did the process get so screwed up at the beginning that Joe Blow gets activated and the rest of us don't?"

In addition to the Vessels of Opportunity program, BP launched what I think of as the Scientists of Opportunity program. It tried to hire marine scientists throughout the Gulf region—including the entire marine sciences department at one university—for its own legal defense in the government's Natural Resources Damage Assessment and Restoration program, which will determine how much money in fines BP must pay. The contract offered the scientists $250 an hour for their work, and prohibited them from publishing or sharing their research for a minimum of three years.

We slept on deck to beat the heat, slapping mosquitoes through the night, except for Jimbo. "Ignore 'em," he advised. "They bite you once, then they're gone. If you don't let 'em bite you, they keep after you."

Jimbo's involvement with the spill began almost from the moment he heard about it while fishing with his old pal Jimmy Buffett in the Bahamas. "We just kept wondering what we could do," Jimbo told me. "It's like the story of the little girl on the beach. The beach was littered with thousands of starfish. And the girl was throwing them back. And a guy asked her if she really thought she could make a difference. And she tossed her starfish in the water and said, 'I did to that one.'"

Jimbo is, among many other things, co-owner of Dragonfly Boatworks in Vero Beach, which makes some of the most enlightened fly-fishing craft ever conceived by humankind. In May, Jimbo and Buffett hatched a plan, with Buffett donating forty-three thousand dollars for the design and construction by Dragonfly of two skiffs custom-made for wildlife rescue. The Shallow Water Attention Terminal, or SWAT, boats have sea-green hulls (so they merge with the waterline and don't spook birds), whisper-soft trolling motors, a draft of just ten inches, mid-deck worktables, misting systems, and canopies.

To operate the boats, Jimbo had to take the Coast Guard training program, just like the VOO operators. He was unimpressed. "You gotta keep your sleeves rolled down at all times. You s'posed to carry a five-gallon bucket onboard. If you take a leak off the side of the boat, your ass is fired."

My VOO mole confirmed this, along with the reality: "I hate to be the bearer of bad news, but if you've gotta go to the bathroom in the middle of Mobile Bay on a boat like mine, you're going to go somewhere, whether you're doing number one, number two, or number three."

After the boats were built, Jimbo was informed by the U.S. Fish and Wildlife Service that if he or anyone else on the boats other than a trained specialist with a federal permit handled an oiled bird, they would be in violation of federal law under the Migratory Bird Treaty Act. Fine, said Jimbo, they would donate the boats to the local Audubon Center and let them do it. Bird experts, after all. Nope, he was told. Audubon Centers don't have permits either. "Most frustrating thing I've ever experienced," Jimbo said.

And Jimbo has experienced a lot. Virtually everyone I spoke with on the Gulf Coast said, "Oh, you have to meet Jimbo Meador. He's the real-life Forrest Gump." The truth is more complicated. Yes, Jimbo's buddy Winston Groom dedicated his famous book to Jimbo. And yes, like Gump, Jimbo ran a huge shrimping business in Alabama. And yes, to get Tom Hanks's accent right, the producers recorded long conversations with Jimbo. ("But I don't know why he bothered," Jimbo said, "because in the movie he sounded like an idiot.") But there the similarity ends. Jimbo has been known to introduce himself by saying, "My name is Jimbo Meador, and I am not retarded." Groom simply used Jimbo's homespun wisdom and good fortune as the inspiration for his character.

"I been blessed," Jimbo admitted. He did well shrimping, but one day he quit and sold his business. "The bycatch was really starting to bother me." He began guiding and teaching fly-fishing for Orvis back in the day when it was just a catalog. Though it seems hard to believe now, at the time the company had little presence in the South. "They didn't even sell short-sleeve shirts!" Jimbo remembered. So he pitched them on selling the Orvis lifestyle, eventually becoming regional manager throughout the Gulf states. Jimbo determined the zip codes that ordered the most merchandise and built stores there. He received 8 percent of every sale. Now he spends most of his time doing things like hunting on Tom McGuane's ranch and fly-fishing with Buffett. Unless he's catching dinner, he has switched to barbless hooks. ("Before I knew some of those fish I released weren't going to make it.")

At dawn, Jimbo arose, stretched, muttered, "I got to marinate," and threw himself overboard. The water looked clear of oil, so I did too, and immediately got stung by a jellyfish. "I used to swim long-distance," Jimbo said, doing long, beautiful strokes around the boat. "I'd go for miles and get stung constantly by jellyfish. You got to put yourself in a different mind-set. They don't actually hurt."

I tried to summon that mind-set as Bill Finch and I kayaked to Petit Bois. We beached the kayak and made our way through the dunes toward the beachside. Blooming white morning glory vines crawled over the sand and scrub. Bill nibbled on wild plants as we walked. He showed me sea rocket, a briny, mustardy green that was a dead ringer for Grey Poupon, and glasswort, which was crunchy and salty, the potato chip of the beach.

Birds flushed out of our path as we walked. Wind whistled through the dunes. The lonesome Gulf Islands have a poignant feel. "Prepare yourself for enchantment!" the *Exploring Gulf Islands National Seashore* guidebook says about Petit Bois. "The first time you cross Mississippi Sound in summer and see this island materialize on the shimmering horizon, you will wonder why you waited so long for such an experience . . . The feeling is primeval, as if you have been deposited on an oasis."

Things had changed. On the beach, the blue tents were still unoccupied. ATV tracks cut into the sand. Stippling the high-tide line were tens of thousands of tar patties, and suddenly we weren't having a nice nature walk anymore. They looked like underbaked molasses ginger cookies. They smelled like hot asphalt. Some were the size of Frisbees. A ghost crab was mining one patty, bringing clawfuls back to his nest.

The others caught up to us and we walked the beach, documenting the oil and the cleanup efforts. A helicopter dipped low to take a good look at us. A flock of brown pelicans sailed past. "Hope you make it, boys," Jimbo said.

The temperature climbed toward one hundred degrees. We trudged down the shadeless beach. The oil seemed to have an affinity for trash. Any piece of plastic was shellacked with it, as if it had some sort of molecular attraction to its own kind. Despite the horror on the beach, the water looked clear. Jimbo needed to marinate. We swam. Jimbo bronzed. He is deeply suspicious of sunscreen. "I hate it," he said. "When your farts start smelling like sunscreen, you know something's wrong." We stood in the surf and watched clouds of mullet dart by. "Shit," said Jimbo, "one throw of my cast net and we'd have supper for a week." But all waters were closed to fishing. On the boat we were eating tins of Portuguese sardines. The dolphins had no such restrictions on them. They caught the breaks like experts, surfing into eighteen inches of water and scraping their bellies on the sand as they scarfed up fish. "Yeah!" said Jimbo, rooting them on. He'd once fished among them in similar shallows. "I was actually surfing a dolphin wake on my paddleboard. My dog was going crazy!"

Farther down the beach, the water turned the color of iced coffee. Blue crabs with aprons full of eggs skittered sideways through it. About a third of the nation's blue crabs come from the Gulf. These "sponge crabs" would soon release their larvae into currents that would take them out into the open Gulf. There, they would spend a month or two feeding on plankton, molting into larger forms, before riding incoming currents back to the estuaries in fall, where they would grow up into proper blue crabs. (Unless they feed somebody else along the way. Crab larvae and juveniles are essential foods for many creatures.) Of course, the toxins in oil accumulate in egg fats and are lethal to larvae. Already, crab larvae with orangish oil droplets trapped inside their shells were being found across the Gulf. "In my forty-two years of studying crabs, I've never seen this," said Harriet Perry of the Gulf Coast Research Laboratory. These particular eggs wouldn't be going anywhere.

Suddenly a pack of Gators—heavy-duty, four-wheel-drive ATVs made by John Deere—came skidding around the end of the island toward us. The cleanup crews were awake. "You know it's against the law to drive a vehicle on the beach," Jimbo said. "And look at this shit." The Gators sped past us toward the shade of the tents. One of the workers was immense. "Damn, that's a big fella!" Jimbo said. "He got to go to the crossroads to turn around!" The crews suited up in Tyvek and gloves and grabbed rakes and plastic trash bags. Many of the workers were obese, and it looked punishingly hot in those suits. One Gator veered toward us and slammed to a stop.

"How'd y'all get here?" the driver asked in a thick Mississippi accent.

"Boat," said Josh.

"Hell, I know that," said the driver. "But how'd you get *here*?"

"Walked." We'd come about a mile down the beach.

The marvel of it all slowly sank in. "You *walked*?"

On the back seat of the Gator, a weary-looking man with a grizzled beard narrowed his eyes at us. "Y'all better not be steppin' on any tar balls," he said. This was the crew boss in charge of cleanup operations on Petit Bois. Things were not going well. He had orders to keep all the Gators operating in a single track, to avoid tearing up the dunes, but now the rut was so deep that the Gators were starting to run aground, breaking down as sand got into their wheel wells. "It's just killing our Gators," he said. How were they supposed to get up and down the island without the Gators?

So far, the crew had raked up sixty tons of oil, deposited it in plastic garbage bags (also made of petroleum), and hauled them out to the barges. But the surge from Tropical Storm Alex had recently deposited a whole new layer of oil on the beach, so they were essentially right back where they'd started. Worse, the new sand deposited by Alex had covered huge mats of old oil, which they now had to dig through several inches of beach to find. The boss was trying to requisition some gas-powered leaf blowers to help blow the new sand off the oiled sand.

Nothing was happening fast. Federal guidelines are strict about heat safety. During a yellow-flag day—pretty much the best you can hope for on the Gulf Coast in summer—employees work forty minutes, then get a twenty-minute rest period. We were into the red-flag days (heat index over 100), meaning twenty minutes on and forty minutes off. Should a black-flag day (heat index above 110) rear its sweaty head, all work would cease. There seemed to be about two hours of functional work per day, and a fair amount of that seemed to be devoted to shuttling people to and from the potties stationed at one end of the six-mile island. "It's a logistical nightmare," the boss sighed. Recently, however, there had been a breakthrough. "We got permission," he said, gesturing out to sea, "to take a pee in the ocean."

As Bill and I kayaked back to our boat, he seemed silent and gloomy. When I asked him about it later, he said, "You know, Petit Bois is such a quiet, retiring place, so unconnected to the rest of the world, where you can't hear anything but the tingle of the sand. To come over the dunes and suddenly see that regimental deployment of tents and chairs, it kind of makes you stiffen up. And then the beach, spotted like a dog yard with all that brown crap, and the ghost crabs tunneling through it, and the waves turning up tar balls instead of shells and pebbles, and before you can digest that, suddenly you see that long line of machines rolling toward you. I can't get over the feeling that the island's been violated twice, first by the oil and then by the assault to save it.

"I don't know what the long-term impacts of the cleanup will be. The tar balls are pretty weathered already, so I don't expect they're radiating toxins as long as they sit undisturbed. But every time a crab or a worm or a bird or a raccoon digs through one or turns it over to see what it is, it will open up the core, exposing those toxic short-chain carbon compounds, and that results in another spurt of contamination. Will that be enough to alter the ecosystem in a big way? We're just going to have to wait a long while to see. The only thing that I'm fairly certain of is that I'll be finding chunks of oil on Petit Bois for years, probably for as long as I'm able to keep going there. And I'm going to have to think about it and worry about it every time I see it. And that just pisses me off."

After Petit Bois, we sailed to the west end of Dauphin Island, anchoring near Katrina Cut—a rift in the island opened up by the hurricane. These barrier islands, which are a mere three thousand years old—"not two generations of cypress" in Bill Finch's terms—get regularly knocked about by storms. Two rigs near our anchorage beeped annoyingly through the night, and the next morning, when Jimbo and I looked to marinate, a strange black slick of congealed matter was drifting past the boat, so we raised anchor and headed for Grand Bay.

We were still hoping to find the old soul of the Gulf, but it found us first. Looming beyond Grand Bay, a black bank of cloud sucked the color out of the western sky and rose imperiously into the troposphere, flicking tongues of lightning at the sea. The water turned a psychotic green. A mitt of wind came across the surface and swatted *Dolphin's Waltz* like a toy. "Better put the sugar to bed," said Jimbo. We could see the Alabama shrimp fleet hauling ass for the shelter of Bayou La Batre, their hulls glowing white against the charcoal sky.

If Josh had said to me at that moment that the time had come to stop playing this eighteenth-century game, to turn on the motor and play it safe, I would have bowed to his experience. But he surprised me. We came about and raised the biggest sail we had, a green spinnaker that billowed in front of the boat like a parachute, and we headed directly away from the storm, riding its thirty-knot gusts toward Mobile Bay.

The storm had decided our speed and direction. We were going home. I stood in the bow and let the cool rain needle my skin. Waves hissed against the hull and splashed me. I held the handrail tight. Horsepower had easily trumped wind power, leaving us as the only boat under way in that half of Mississippi Sound. The frothing waves obscured the horizon, and I could see nothing but sails and water and cloud.

We sailed for hours on that course. The difference between powerboating and sailing is profound, but it's a feeling that only sneaks up on you once you've been at it awhile. It's a cool, crisp, minty serenity caused, paradoxically, by a lack of control over your fate. You can't choose your weather. You can't bend the world to your will.

Entering Mobile Bay, we jibed to pick up the shipping channel, and the full brunt of the wind came across our deck. Josh's eyes flicked from the wind to the spinnaker to our course. "Harden up on that sheet a bit!" he said. Bill winched in the sheet, the spinnaker snapped into place, and *Dolphin's Waltz* heeled over and locked into a groove. We surged forward, thirty-five thousand pounds of wood and fiberglass and lead cleaving water from her bow into two foamy curls.

"She got a bone in her mouth now!" Jimbo shouted from the wheel.

The channel from Mobile Bay into the Mobile Yacht Club harbor is six-and-a-half feet deep, more or less, quickly dropping to five if you stray. *Dolphin's Waltz* draws six feet of water. When she is heeled over, flying across a strong wind, she draws a little less. Keep her at full speed, hard into the wind, and she can sneak through five-plus feet of water. Then again, when a boat with that much mass runs aground at that speed, very bad things happen.

The bridge loomed. "Jimbo," Josh said, "you just keep her pointed exactly at that top span." I asked Josh when he wanted to drop the sails. He waggled his head. "It's all about the braggin' rights, Dawg."

I stationed myself on the bowsprit in classic King of the World position, the bay sluicing underneath me as the bridge towered over us. We had ten feet of clearance above our mast and about that on either side of the channel. "We comin' in hot!" Josh yelled.

Suddenly a powerboat came out of the harbor straight at us. "Boat!" I shouted, gripping the handrail.

"We got right of way!" Josh yelled back. "We got rights over *everybody* right now!"

Sure enough, the powerboat scrambled sideways like a pedestrian dodging a runaway truck, and we blew into the harbor with our green chute flying, past a handful of frozen onlookers on the dock. One of them snapped out of it, pointed, and shouted, "Josh, that's the coolest thing you have *ever* done!"

Josh grinned. Then we doused the sails, fired up the diesel, and motored back into our slot.

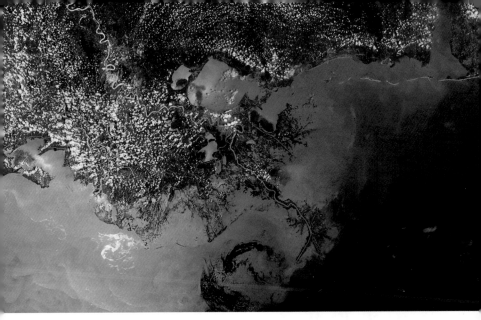

The oil spill in the Gulf of Mexico in July 2010. The Mississippi River cuts through this picture from upper left to lower right, terminating in its "bird's foot" delta. Black swirls of oil can be seen to the left and right of this delta, mingling with the muddy, light-tan waters closer to shore. Lake Pontchartrain is in the upper middle of the photograph. New Orleans lies on its southern shore on several bends in the river. The MR. GO canal extends southeast from the city to the Gulf. The Atchafalaya River empties into the large bay to the lower left. The arrow-shaped bay in the upper right corner is Mobile Bay. The barrier islands of Mississippi and Alabama stretch west from the edge of Mobile Bay. Petit Bois Island is the middle, boomerang-shaped island. Grand Bay is on the coast northeast of Petit Bois. PHOTO COURTESY NASA

Oil oozing out of the sand on Grand Isle, Louisiana.

PHOTO BY ROWAN JACOBSEN

The author and Bill Finch getting blasted by an airboat in Grand Bay.
PHOTO BY ANDY ANDERSON

Oiled boom and
marsh grass off
the coast of Ocean
Springs, Mississippi.
PHOTO BY
ROWAN JACOBSEN

An island rookery
near the Nature
Conservancy's oyster
reef restoration site,
before the oil arrived.
PHOTO BY
ROWAN JACOBSEN

Dolphin's Waltz passing a gas platform in Mississippi Sound.
PHOTO BY ANDY ANDERSON

Tar ball on Petit
Bois Island.
PHOTO BY
ROWAN JACOBSEN

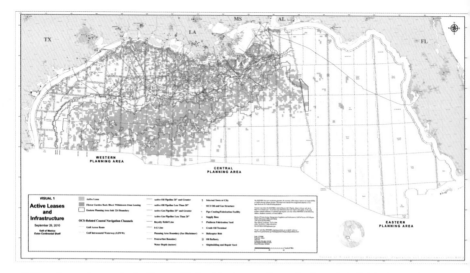

Oil and gas rigs and platforms (light blue), pipelines (red and dark blue), and leases (green), in the Gulf of Mexico as of September 2010. IMAGE COURTESY BUREAU OF OCEAN ENERGY MANAGEMENT, REGULATION AND ENFORCEMENT

Dispersant and oil mixing on the Gulf surface.
PHOTO COURTESY PROJECT GULF IMPACT

Coast Guard sign warning boaters against the use of dispersant. This sign was posted in marinas throughout the Gulf Coast.

PHOTO BY DON ABRAMS

One of the rare deep-sea corals (with red brittle sea star attached) killed by the sunken oil. The researchers state, "Although the orange tips on some branches of the coral [are] the color of living tissue, it is unlikely that any living tissue remains on this animal." PHOTO COURTESY LOPHELIA II 2010, NOAA OER, AND BOEMRE

The disappearance
of Isle Derniére.
IMAGE COURTESY
STATE OF LOUISIANA

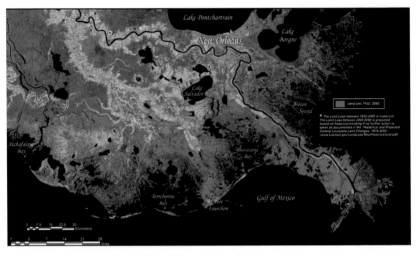

Documented and projected land loss in southern Louisiana, 1932–2050.
IMAGE COURTESY U.S. GEOLOGICAL SURVEY

Canals cut through the
Louisiana marshes by
the oil and gas industry.
PHOTO COURTESY STATE
OF LOUISIANA

Living cypress swamp, southern Mississippi.

PHOTO BY DON ABRAMS

Dead cypress swamp, now a salt marsh, near Dulac, Louisiana.

PHOTO BY ROWAN JACOBSEN

Virgil Dardar at his Isle de Jean Charles house, wrecked by Hurricane Gustav.
PHOTO BY ROWAN JACOBSEN

The road to Isle de Jean Charles, collapsing fast.
PHOTO BY ROWAN JACOBSEN

Electrical line to Isle de Jean Charles. These poles were on dry ground thirty years ago. PHOTO BY ROWAN JACOBSEN

Chapter 7

OF EELS, WHALES,
AND REPERCUSSIONS

STEP AWAY FROM the Gulf with me for a moment, to the icy ink of Maine's Damariscotta River, where an eel stirs. On this moonless September night, silvery strands of starlight twirl in the riffles. The eel is twenty years old, and she has lived in the Damariscotta, nipping small river bugs from the rocks and riverbed, for nearly all that time. But now the cold of the water and the new moon and her own internal clock tell her that it's time to leave.

She wriggles downstream, surfing the currents, and she isn't alone. All around her, snaking through the black waters, are others of her kind. The river is a braid of eels, swimming for the sea.

From the Gulf of Maine, the eel turns south and begins a thousand-mile, many-month journey across the Atlantic, to a swirling gyre in the ocean south of Bermuda. There, the surface is covered with a tangled mat of leafy, yellow-brown seaweed, floating on grapelike air pods. The eel has reached the Sargasso Sea.

For centuries, sailors have described the eerie stillness of the Sargasso Sea, that patch in the center of the Atlantic that's always covered in sargassum mats. Ships that were captured by the sargassum, they believed, could never escape. Ghost ships, they whispered, lay waiting, their hulls draped in a living yellow net.

Recently, though, researchers learned something even more astounding than any sea story. The two-thousand-mile-long Sargasso Sea is also the breeding ground for every Atlantic and European eel on Earth.

When our eel reaches the edge of the seaweed, she dives and slides into its mass, joining a darting, wriggling, pulsing community of small creatures. She spawns, ejecting eggs from her underbelly onto the sargassum. Stuck to the fronds, the eggs will hatch in a few days and the larval eels will join the community, dodging predators in leafy safety until they begin their own epic journey, drifting with the currents back to the rivers of the eastern seaboard.

Sargassum is found in places besides the Sargasso Sea. Those light brown ridges of seaweed you've stepped over at the high tide line, with little poppable pods and masses of tiny crustaceans inside, were probably sargassum. But because so much of it pools permanently in its eponymous sea, we always assumed that was where it all came from.

But it isn't. Two years ago, researchers confirmed that sargassum doesn't reproduce in the cold Atlantic at all. Almost every strand of it is born in the Gulf of Mexico.

Sargassum's great breeding ground is in the nutrient-rich Gulf waters not far from where the *Deepwater Horizon* exploded. There, it has been continuously dividing itself for thousands, if not millions, of years. Drifting with the winds and currents, it spreads across the Gulf, catching the Loop Current, a marine highway that traces a horseshoe through the Gulf before ducking between Florida and Cuba and curling out into the Atlantic. One branch of the current glances off other Atlantic gyres and swirls into a vortex, and there it stays. (The same dynamics are also responsible for the Atlantic Garbage Patch, a vortex of floating plastic trash.)

By steadily feeding Gulf sargassum to the Sargasso Sea, the Gulf of Mexico is responsible for every eel in the Damariscotta, every eel in Galicia, every eel in the dark mutinous Shannon waves. Yet the sargassum in the Gulf took a direct hit from the oil slick. "They're in the same spot," the University of South Alabama's Sean Powers, an expert on the plant, told the *New York Times*. When it gets coated in oil, seaweed can't breathe or absorb light, and it dies. As do its inhabitants, said Powers. "Once it's oiled, from everything we know of the effects of oil, all of those animals that live in the sargassum will die."

And that means a lot more than just eels. Long before oil rigs were generously providing the fish of the Gulf with cover, massive sargassum mats were creating intricate habitat for its residents, a kind of open-ocean, floating analog to the coastal wetlands. Shrimp, crabs, sea horses, and baby fish all hide in its labyrinth. "It's the only structure out there that provides them any refuge from predators," Powers said. Besides the eels, everything from tuna to sea turtles spawns in the sargassum, gluing their eggs to the leaves. Overall, at least 5 species of turtles, 19 types of birds, 100 species of fish, and 145 species of invertebrates depend on this homely yellow weed.

No one knows whether the oil spill will decimate eel populations in America and Europe as less sargassum finds its way to the Atlantic. It's conceivable. The real point is that nobody knows. The little tale of the eels and the seaweed is a classic example of the incredible complexity of ecosystems—and of how little we understand them. For every relationship we've teased out, like that of the Gulf of Mexico, the sargassum, and the eels, there are a thousand others we haven't yet suspected.

For example, in the 1920s, researchers playing around with the new technology of sonar noticed that their sound waves kept bouncing off a seemingly hard surface about 3,300 feet beneath the waves. The ocean was deeper than that; this seemed like some sort of false bottom. This deep-scattering layer, as they called it, was found throughout nearly every ocean in the world. Most mysterious of all, it rose toward the surface at night, then dropped back down with the dawn. Not until 1948 did we prove that the deep-scattering layer was alive—a thin sheet of seafood, miles long but only a few feet thick, dense enough to reflect sound, composed of billions of fish stretching across the abyssal depths. Hiding in the dark by day, they rise at dusk to feed on phytoplankton closer to the surface. And they make up a sizable portion of the ocean's biomass. Dolphins, sperm whales, and bluefin tuna all dive to feed on the deep-scattering layers, of which there are several, each occupying a different depth. (One of the world's largest communities of sperm whales lives in the Gulf, not far from the Macondo well, because the fishing in its deep-scattering layer is so fine.) Living in eternal night, the deep-scattering layers are off the radar of all but a few human beings. Yet they contain so much life, so many species. And those species connect to so many others. And quite a few of those connections eventually lead to us.

We are only beginning to understand the intricate workings of the ocean. In 2010, researchers learned of a new biological mechanism that helps bring essential nutrients from the deep ocean up to the surface, significantly enhancing phytoplankton production, thus making more fish. It's called the "whale pump," but a more accurate name would be the "whale poop pump." Whales dive to the seafloor, eat squid and other sea life, then return to the surface to breathe. While there, they relieve themselves, emitting great clouds of nutrient-rich guano— exactly what phytoplankton require. By recovering nutrients from the seafloor and enriching the surface waters, whales make more fish. Remove the whales, and you lose the tiny surface life as well.

Every time we learn something like this, we need to remind ourselves that natural systems are much more finely tuned than we think, and if we like the way they currently work, then we should try very, very hard not to screw with them.

On August 4, three weeks after BP managed to cap its runaway well and stop oil from flowing into the Gulf, White House energy czar and former EPA director Carol Browner told Matt Lauer on NBC's *Today Show* that "more than three quarters of the oil is gone. It was captured, it was skimmed, it was burned, it was contained. Mother Nature did her part." Displaying a sort of medieval understanding of biology, Browner explained that "some of it will become very small microorganisms and disappear into the Gulf."

Okay, Browner's no scientist, but she was relying on a National Oceanic and Atmospheric Administration (NOAA) report, which seemed to have been designed to be as opaque as possible. Its "BP Deepwater Horizon Oil Budget" indicated that, of the 205 million gallons of spilled oil, 25 percent had evaporated or dissolved, 17 percent had been directly recovered from the wellhead, 16 percent had been naturally dispersed, 8 percent had been chemically dispersed, 5 percent had been burned, 3 percent had been skimmed, and the remaining 26 percent was "residual"—having hit shore or was still floating on or near the surface.

By my reckoning, I'd call one quarter of the oil "gone," rather than Browner's "more than three quarters." A total of 25 percent was captured, skimmed, and burned. Why the government was interpreting this as good news I can't imagine. That all those thousands of Vessels of Opportunity and professional skimming vessels had managed to skim only 3 percent of the oil strikes me as a debacle of the first order. That 5 percent was sent into the atmosphere in toxic clouds is no more heartening.

Even NOAA's characterization of the rest of the oil displayed a healthy dose of wishful thinking. The 16 percent that had been "naturally dispersed" had simply been emulsified, like a well-shaken salad dressing, when it shot out of the wellhead and hit the water with intense force. It and the 8 percent that had been "chemically dispersed" were still lurking in tiny droplets throughout the water column, too small to float to the surface. "Dispersion increases the likelihood that the oil will be biodegraded," the report explained—in other words, oil-eating microbes would break it down. But even NOAA was forced to admit that "until it is biodegraded, naturally or chemically dispersed oil, even in dilute amounts, can be toxic to vulnerable species." In fact, the dispersant used by BP is as toxic as crude, and even more toxic when mixed with crude. BP's decision to spray two million gallons of it into the oil—some at the surface, some at the wellhead, a mile deep—was one of the most controversial parts of the *Deepwater Horizon* tragedy. Dispersant is industrial-strength detergent. Just like the stuff you use on your dishes, it acts to break up oils and fats into tiny droplets that can wash away. But the stuff used to disperse an oil slick is far stronger than anything we would use at home. The first product used, Corexit 9527, includes a solvent called 2-butoxyethanol, which is suspected of causing respiratory, nervous, liver, kidney, and blood disorders. After BP quickly burned through the world's entire stockpile of Corexit 9527, it switched to Corexit 9500, which doesn't contain 2-butoxyethanol. Overall, very little is known about dispersants' toxic effect on humans or marine life, but they are suspect enough that the U.K. has already banned their use along shorelines.

Equally troubling is the portion of the oil characterized by NOAA as "dissolved," meaning it had broken down into microscopic oil molecules and merged with the water "just as sugar can be dissolved in water." Well, just because sugar dissolves in water doesn't mean it's gone. Invisible, perhaps, but not gone. The notion that "out of sight" equals "gone" has underpinned centuries of environmental abuse. The Gulf itself has taken a fair share of this abuse as the farms, factories, and cities of the Midwest flushed their wastes down the great disposal chute of the Mississippi. Chicago rejiggered its rivers a century ago so that its sewage would flow into the Mississippi and out of mind instead of surfacing in Lake Michigan like Banquo's ghost. Illinois's problems became Missouri's, Missouri's Louisiana's, and Louisiana's the Gulf's.

By spraying million of gallons of dispersant into the oil spill, and by counting on Mother Nature to do her part on the majority of the oil, BP and NOAA dispelled most of the oil to the mythical land of Away and declared victory. This was about as enlightened as the Gulf sportfishermen who sink their empty beer bottles to dispose of them. Gone!

In truth, a massive amount of the oil that Browner had pronounced "gone" was actually lurking three thousand to four thousand feet beneath the surface—on a collision course with the deep-scattering layer—in vast "plumes" spreading out from the wellhead in several directions. "Plumes" was the word used by Samantha Joye, the University of Georgia marine scientist who first discovered them, and "plume" was the word that stuck, but it was a bit misleading. NOAA, once it eventually acknowledged the existence of these phenomena, referred to them as "diffuse clouds." Whatever you call them, the oil in these clouds was so disperse—about 1 part per million—that if you'd breaststroked through one, you'd never have noticed.

Still, when such a phenomenon is the size of Manhattan—twenty miles long, a mile wide, and 650 feet high—that adds up to a lot of oil. The plumes contained at least forty million gallons of oil, along with twice that much natural gas. The visible cleanup efforts were little more than window dressing. The bulk of the oil dove deep, spreading throughout the northern Gulf.

BP's deus ex machina was oil-eating microbes. This hope was behind Browner's odd "some of it will become very small microorganisms and disappear into the Gulf" statement. Small amounts of oil seep into all the oceans of the world through natural fissures in the seafloor, and every ocean contains bacteria that have evolved to live off that concentrated food source. Like tiny internal-combustion engines, they can burn hydrocarbons for energy. Because about twenty-one million gallons of crude seep into the Gulf each year (about twice the *Exxon Valdez* spill, and one tenth the BP spill), it contains more active oil-eating bacteria than any other body of water. These bacteria live throughout the Gulf, hanging on at low levels until some crude shows up, at which point they eat, reproduce, eat, reproduce, and so on, cranking up their numbers into a population explosion that lasts as long as the crude does.

The bacteria were BP's best hope in the Gulf, and sure

enough, they did their part. By August, according to a study by Department of Energy scientists published in *Science*, the plume had disappeared. Bacterial concentrations in the vicinity were twice as high as concentrations outside the area. These bacteria—some ten thousand species—included some that specialized in eating petroleum in the forty-degree depths where the plumes were found. They were full of hydrocarbonoclastic enzymes—the molecular tools used to dismantle hydrocarbons into digestible components. Hence the little dance party in NOAA's cubicles. Oily plumes transformed into oil-eating bacteria! Problem solved!

Except. Anyone with even the most elementary knowledge of food webs knows that it won't stop with the bacteria—and researchers at Alabama's Dauphin Island Sea Lab proved it. Much of the carbon in crude oil is in the form of a particularly light isotope that is different from the carbon found in the atmosphere and in living plants and animals. By analyzing the carbon found in the zooplankton (the tiniest animals) in the Gulf during the weeks after the oil spill, the researchers showed that a massive amount of the oil that reached shallow waters did in fact get eaten by bacteria, which were then eaten by zooplankton, which still contained the "shadow" of the oil in their bodies. From there, the shadow continued to pass up into larger creatures.

And what about the shadow of the neurotoxins and carcinogens also found in crude? In June, the waters off Louisiana's Grand Isle tested off the charts in polycyclic aromatic hydrocarbons (PAHs), the most toxic, and feared, compounds in crude. PAHs are the things that give people cancer. "There was a huge increase of PAHs that are bioavailable to the organisms—and that means they can essentially be uptaken by organisms throughout the food chain," said Kim Anderson, the Oregon State

University toxicologist who did the study. The fortyfold surge in PAH levels was the largest Anderson had ever seen. Ironically, by breaking apart the particles, the dispersants may have made the PAHs far more bioavailable, just as they did to the oil itself.

Did this make Gulf seafood toxic? Not if you ask the Food and Drug Administration. In one press release, it explained that "experts trained in a rigorous sensory analysis process have been testing Gulf seafood for the presence of contaminants, and every seafood sample from reopened waters has passed sensory testing for contamination with oil and dispersant." Sounds pretty impressive. I'd eat seafood with confidence after hearing that. But not once I learned that the "rigorous sensory analysis" consisted of some guys in a Pascagoula, Mississippi, lab taking a sniff of a few pieces of shrimp and oysters from various regions of the Gulf. I kid you not. When President Obama said on June 15, "Let me be clear. Seafood from the Gulf today is safe to eat," and proceeded to chow down on crab cakes and fried shrimp, he was relying on sniff tests. "Properly trained noses are really remarkable organs," explained Brian Gorman, NOAA's spokesperson for the program. Maybe so, but not all the shit in that food chain necessarily stinks. In June, NOAA had fifty-five trained sniff inspectors and was shuttling another fifty-five through emergency training. These professional noses sniff a tiny fraction of the seafood being fished out of the Gulf; 99.99 percent of it goes straight from the boats to the docks unsniffed.

And even as NOAA's seafood sommeliers kept giving Gulf shrimp two thumbs up, it kept flunking independent tests by scientists using more than their schnozzes. Gulf shrimp ordered by a Florida television station and tested in a New Jersey lab contained amounts of two PAH compounds—phenanthrene and anthracene—well beyond the FDA limits. And tests conducted by Dr. William Sawyer, of Toxicology Consultants and Assessment Specialists, found widespread contamination. "We've collected shrimp, oysters, and finfish on their way to marketplace," he said. "We tested a good number of seafood samples and in 100 percent we found petroleum." Sawyer went on to state the obvious: "The sensory test employed by the FDA detects compounds that are volatile that have an odor; we're detecting compounds that are low volatility and are very low odor. We found not only petroleum in the digestive tracts [of shrimp], but also in the edible portions of fish." His conclusion? "I don't recommend eating Gulf seafood, not with the risk of liver and kidney damage. The reason FDA has not made that advisory is because they've relied on this sensory test. You may as well send inspectors out to look at the fish and say they look nice. They're sniffing for something they can't detect."

Eventually, as alarm built about the inadequacy of sniff tests, NOAA and the FDA bowed to pressure and began doing chemical testing. They tested a grand total of twenty-one shrimp in Mississippi, and forty-two each in Alabama and Florida, before opening those states' waters to shrimping in September—despite the fact that fishermen were still seeing slicks in the water. In fact, the actual levels of PAHs found in shrimp caught off the coast of Pensacola were high enough that, if they'd been found in fish, the waters would have been kept closed to fishing until more tests could be done. But the FDA, clearly never having dined along the Gulf Coast, assumed that people eat only half as much shrimp as they do fish, and thus allowed higher levels of PAHs in shrimp. In addition, the amount of PAHs allowed in Gulf seafood was more than three times higher than what had been allowed in seafood affected by oil spills off the west coast a decade earlier, for two reasons, as the FDA explained. One, it had raised the acceptable risk of developing cancer from the PAHs from 1 in a million to 1 in 100,000. Two, people were now larger than they were during those earlier spills.

Perhaps the most important point to take away from the FDA's shenanigans is that all Gulf shrimp tested contained some PAHs. Thanks to us, oil is everywhere and in everything.

And now, so are dispersant compounds. Chemical testing for those—which are generally considered more toxic than crude oil compounds—didn't begin until November, long after the FDA had been declaring Gulf seafood completely safe. Five times the amount of dispersant compounds was allowed in shrimp, crabs, and oysters as in finfish.

In general, levels of dispersant compounds were low in tested seafood, but how much is safe? How much cadmium, copper, lead, and mercury—all of which is present in crude oil, but none of which is tested for—is safe? As of fall 2010, neither NOAA, nor the FDA, nor any other agency seemed to have the credibility to convincingly answer this.

The fantasy that oil-eating bacteria would make our problems go away didn't last long. In late August, not three weeks after the Department of Energy's report on the competitive-eating-champion bacteria in *Science*, Samantha Joye reported her discovery of a two-inch-thick mat of oil resting on vast swathes of the bottom of the Gulf, covering a layer of dead invertebrates such as marine worms and shrimp. A separate University of South Florida team discovered oil droplets coating sediment in DeSoto Canyon, an exceptionally productive part of the Gulf near the Florida Panhandle. And a team from Columbia University reported "oily snow" half a foot thick in some places, along with discolored zooplankton.

On September 16 came clarity, with yet another report in *Science*, this one from David Valentine at U.C. Santa Barbara, announcing that what the microbes had been feasting on was not oil but natural gas—which outnumbered oil in the plumes two to one, turning the deep sea into a sort of toxic petroleum seltzer. The microbes were concentrating on propane and ethane, some of the smallest molecules found in crude, while leaving larger oil molecules intact.

Apparently the microbes hadn't cleaned their plates quite as much as NOAA and BP had hoped. Samantha Joye called NOAA's accounting of where the oil had gone "a joke, a fairy tale scenario." "I understand why people want [the oil] to disappear," she said, "but who in their right mind would believe that? It makes absolutely no sense."

The oil "did not disappear," concurred Florida State University oceanographer Ian MacDonald. "It sank." Whether broken up by dispersant or natural pressure into microscopic droplets, it hadn't had enough buoyancy to float. Instead, it seemed to have triggered an unprecedented blizzard of "sea snot," as described by the U.C. Santa Barbara researchers, who had traps on the bottom of the Gulf monitoring such things. When phytoplankton are stressed, they produce mucus, which causes them to stick to each other and any other nearby tiny particles, including oil droplets. As the slimy clumps of phytoplankton die and lose their buoyancy, they fall to the bottom, taking a great deal of the microscopic life in the water column with them. This lost generation of plankton leads to a lost generation of larval fish, and on up the food chain. Whether the Gulf ecosystem can compensate for this lost generation in the future is unknown.

Meanwhile, the Coast Guard and its scientists continued to blunder along in Inspector Clouseau mode, seemingly the only investigators in the Gulf who couldn't find any oil. "We have, to date, not found anything that is: one, unexpected; two, particularly alarming; and three, that is recoverable," Coast Guard science adviser Stephen Lehmann announced in October, dismissing the idea that Louisiana light sweet crude could sink. "Even when it gets very old, even when a lot of it evaporates, it doesn't get to a point where it wants to sink. It's very light, in fact I don't know that we know of a crude oil that sinks in salt water. There are refined oils that do that, but with crude oils I can't think of one. So the concept of a big slick of oil sinking to the bottom is kind of an anathema. We have not found anything that we would consider actionable at 5,000 feet or 5 feet."

Tell that to the shrimpers who returned in November from a three-hour drag in recently reopened Louisiana waters with their nets and shrimp covered in oil and tar balls (which caused the government to do an about-face and reclose thousands of square miles of reopened fishing grounds). Shrimp live on the bottom of the sea, exactly where the sunken oil would be—a chilling thought for the Gulf shrimp industry.

You had to wonder whether the Coast Guard scientists were actually searching in the wrong gulf, because even as the Coast Guard was holding its press conference, Penn State marine biologist Charles Fisher, using a deep-sea submersible, was finding "an underwater graveyard" of deepwater corals a few miles from the well and at a similar depth. Instead of vivid, Technicolor reefs, he found "a field of brown corals with exposed skeleton—white, brittle stars tightly wound around the skeleton, not waving their arms like they usually do." The coral, spread across thirty sites, was all recently dead or still slowly dying from exposure to something very toxic. "Within minutes of our arrival at this site, it was evident to the biologists on board that this site was unlike any others that we have seen over the course of hundreds of hours of studying the deep corals in the Gulf of Mexico over the last decade with remotely-operated-vehicles and submersibles."

What could do such a thing to these communities? "Even though some are adapted to oil, *none* are adapted to dispersant. If there was a heavy exposure to dispersant in any of the communities, this could have some very serious toxic effects. If in fact the dispersed oil forms small globules, this could foul feeding appendages. It could foul respiratory appendages and have a very bad effect on these communities."

Fisher's conclusion was in stark contrast to the Coast Guard's findings. "We have a smoking gun," he said. "The circumstantial evidence is very strong that it's linked to the spill."

Ironically, many of these deepwater coral communities were unknown until the past few years, when the Minerals Management Service—the same agency dismantled for its pathetic policing of the oil industry—financed extensive exploration of the Gulf floor using robotic submersibles. These explorations have turned up more than a hundred deepwater coral sites sporting numerous new species and wondrous biodiversity. Yet those species may depart before we even get to know them, thanks to the two million gallons of dispersant, which is particularly toxic to coral. "We consider the dispersed oil more harmful than a sheen passing over the reef," said Billy Causey, Southeast regional director for NOAA's National Marine Sanctuaries program. Louisiana State University marine biologist Prosanta Chakrabarty was more blunt: "There are species out there that haven't been described, and they're going to disappear."

In addition to killing deepwater corals, dispersed oil will turn up in crabs, shrimp, and other invertebrates. In general, while fish can detoxify a certain amount of oil and dispersants, the "chemicals accumulate for years in invertebrates," according to the *Journal of the American Medical Association*. By September, University of South Florida researchers were already seeing toxic effects on phytoplankton from carcinogens in the oil and dispersants, which were causing some bacteria to mutate. "The impact on commercially important larvae that are bathed in this stuff is hard to say," USF's John Paul explained. "We might see groupers with tumors three years from now. It's a long process."

It is indeed. The hydrocarbons coating the floor of the Gulf are the heavy compounds, the asphalts and tars made of long chains of carbon atoms—molecules too large to be easily eaten by microbes, especially in that low-oxygen environment. According to University of Louisville microbiologist Ronald Atlas, it will take "weeks to months to years, depending on the compounds and concentrations—not hours or days. Much of the real tar or asphalt compounds are not readily subject to microbial attack . . . Tar tends to persist. Asphalt tends to persist."

Whatever is going on, down there in the wine-dark depths, it is going to keep going on for some time. And it has never happened before quite like this. We have a gigantic experiment under way in the Gulf. While phytoplankton and seaweed struggle to deal with the impact of the oil, bacteria surge. Phytoplankton and bacteria may both be microscopic, but they are not the same thing, and they tend to create different ecosystems. Phytoplankton make their food through photosynthesis and are the natural food for everything from oysters to tiny crustaceans, which pass the energy up the food web to larval fish, then to intermediate predators like mullet and squid, and on to top predators like tuna and whales. Bacteria recycle dead matter (which is what oil is) and are a very different type of food. Yes, as the Dauphin Island Sea Lab discovered, some of those bacteria were consumed by zooplankton and passed into the food web, but what happens to the food web when it changes the foundation of its diet? No one knows. We do know that bacteria are a natural food for jellyfish, which secrete a mucus that feeds bacteria, forming a semi-closed food loop. Other than sea turtles, not many things eat jellyfish, so swapping out phytoplankton for bacteria risks creating a new Gulf based more on jellyfish than on oysters, shrimp, and tuna.

It wouldn't be the first time an ecosystem flipped. As Scripps Institution oceanographer Jeremy Jackson pointed out, "today Chesapeake Bay is a bacterially dominated ecosystem with a totally different trophic structure from a century ago." This "rise of slime" has resulted in a cloudy bay full of bacteria and other organic matter that isn't vacuumed up the food web like it used to be. In the case of the Chesapeake, the villain wasn't oil but over-harvesting of the animals that made the links between phytoplankton and the upper levels of the food web, especially oysters. But these same issues face the Gulf, and the smaller Chesapeake should serve as a wake-up call.

We tend to think of ecosystems as foregone conclusions. If we harm them, it may reduce their vitality, but then if we lay off the abuse, they will eventually bounce back, as long as we don't destroy them completely. Not always. Many variations on an ecosystem can exist in a given place, some of them quite different from one another. They are chaotic systems, like storms, whirlpools, and cities. Sometimes a small change in initial conditions can force surprising changes in function.

My favorite way to think about this is to picture a sailboat. *Dolphin's Waltz* is a system designed to stay vertical. Whenever the wind pushes its sails down, that also lifts the keel up, and those eleven thousand pounds of lead immediately act to bring the boat back to vertical and keep the interior dry. It's a self-reinforcing system. The farther down the sails are pushed, the more gravity tries to restore them. More than one sailor has assumed that things couldn't possibly go otherwise. But if a storm is strong enough, and wind and wave manage to push the hull over so far that the boat swamps, then the system instantly switches to a new state, one that actively resists any efforts to right it, possibly even "turning turtle": complete capsizing.

Ecosystems turn turtle regularly. Iraq, once one of the most fertile regions in the world, the cradle of civilization, became a nearly barren desert after the forests that held its soil and water in place had been removed. The Gulf of Maine, once a cod paradise, became infested with lobster after their primary predator was fished out. The Bay of Campeche, on the Mexican side of the Gulf of Mexico, used to have thriving populations of mangrove oysters. Then the Ixtoc I well blew, spilling about 140 million gallons of oil into the bay in 1979 and depressing populations of larval fish and shellfish for years. In 2010, researchers returned to the Bay of Campeche to assess the effects of the spill thirty years later. At first they couldn't find any mangrove oysters, and they were told by locals that the oysters never came back after the oil spill. Eventually, they discovered one elderly fisherman who still knew where to find a few oysters. He reported that "while he ate them, they tasted fine, but afterwards, a burp would have a taste or smell of oil." Twenty years ago, Alaska's Prince William Sound had one of the most lucrative herring fisheries in the world. Then the *Exxon Valdez* spilled 11 million gallons of oil into the sound, the herring fishery collapsed, the ecosystem spasmed, and most of the herring never returned.

These are worst-case scenarios. The Gulf will not be killed by the BP spill, but it will be *changed*, and probably not for the better. As Ian MacDonald said, "I expect the hydrocarbon imprint of the BP discharge will be detectable in the marine environment for the rest of my life." Stan Senner, director of conservation at the Oceans Conservancy, summed things up in *Discovery News*: "The Gulf of Mexico is not dead. There will be lots of life there, but the ecosystems do change. What comes next may be a different mix of things, some of the more sensitive species may disappear. That would be a tragedy."

Chapter 8

THE LAST DAYS OF
ISLE DE JEAN CHARLES

V IRGIL DARDAR LIVES at the tip of Louisiana's Isle de
Jean Charles, but the government would prefer that he
didn't. Isle de Jean Charles, a three-mile spit of dry ground in
the midst of Terrebonne Parish's vast green wetlands, is the
ancestral home of Virgil and a handful of other families of the
Biloxi-Chitimacha tribe of American Indians. It is also crumbling into the water in real time. Stand at the end, dangle your
toes over the edge, and watch it go. The Barataria-Terrebonne
Estuary, the heart of the Mississippi River Delta, loses another
acre of marshland to the sea every forty-five minutes, and Isle
de Jean Charles bids adieu to more than its fair share.

The paved road to Isle de Jean Charles cuts across three miles
of open water that used to be marsh. Now waves gnaw at it 24-7.
It submerges completely at high tide every time a wind blows
out of the south, emerging a few hours later and a few millimeters smaller. Even at low tide, much of it is down to one jagged
lane. A snaking line of orange cones leads cars along the safest
path. I drove it for the first time in May, with the windows
down and the radio on, following the map as far as I could into

the marshes, listening to ads from lawyers ("You deserve to be compensated for your loss. Don't sign anything until you've called the law offices of ———. Call us now to begin your recovery!") and the Louisiana Seafood Promotion and Marketing Board ("Many fishing areas are still open. Make sure you ask for Louisiana Seafood!").

The island road ends in a row of sorry fishing camps, surrounded by refuse from 2008's Hurricane Gustav. I hit that spot, then turned my car around and bumped into Virgil, who had brown mud splattered across his white T-shirt and was cleaning the same out of his truck. He had a bald head, a white beard, a few random teeth, and the grooved crow's-feet of someone who's been squinting into sunny waters his whole life. He told me to call him Kadoo—virtually everyone in the area goes by nicknames—though when I asked him how to spell it, he wasn't sure. Kadoo was surprisingly chipper, considering he was having one shitty day.

"I been denominated," he said to me in a heavy bayou accent. I had no idea what he was talking about. He yanked a folded piece of paper out of his jeans pocket and handed it to me. It was a ticket from the Louisiana Department of Wildlife and Fisheries. "I fish oysters," he said, which explained the mud. Dredging oysters is a dirty business. "I been fishing oysters for thirty-six years, since I was sixteen." Since the spill, he'd been fishing double-time. "We worked all week soon as we found out. They said the oil move west. What do we do? We're fishermen. We're stuck." His usual oyster grounds, underwater leases near Isle de Jean Charles designated as Areas 15 and 16, were closed because of the spill, so he had been harvesting farther west at Area 17—which Wildlife and Fisheries had also closed, though Kadoo insisted he didn't know that. "It was open! According to the health department, it stays open till six thirty tonight! So here we are, fishin'. And then the bossman call and say, 'Might be the best thing y'all come in.' Okay, we on our way in. Sure enough, Wildlife was there. They shut us down, give us tickets, made us throw our oysters overboard. Ticket like that run you 'bout a thousand dollars. They coulda gave us a warning. Tha's wrong, you know? I mean, what can ya do? The oysters are still good. They ain't no problem with the oysters. For the time being, they ain't no oil around. But it's getting closer in."

In recent years, multiple hurricanes have left the island a disaster zone of smashed homes, beached boats, and dead trees. Most of the siding had been ripped from Kadoo's house and barn, and his barn had been roofless since Gustav. His was the first house on the island to be raised on posts—three feet after Katrina, five feet after Rita—but that didn't help much during Gustav, whose surge inundated the island under ten feet of water. Since no piece of land on the bayou is higher than a few feet, during Gustav the entire area was open sea.

One thing you notice while driving around southern Louisiana is the amazing number of billboards advertising home raising—jacking existing homes up on wooden posts so they'll stay dry in the next hurricanes. It's kind of like people standing on tiptoes to stay dry as their boat sinks, and it's big business, because FEMA will provide thirty thousand dollars in insurance money to raise homes that have been totaled by hurricanes. That's more than it costs the contractors, who charge full price and then split the gravy with the homeowners through a variety of schemes.

But it was too late for Isle de Jean Charles. After Rita in 2005, the state had helped islanders rebuild, but after Gustav in 2008, it wrote off the island, offering to help residents relocate, but not rebuild. "They want us to move off the island," Kadoo told me. "Want to put us in a higher place. But we're not moving. This is where we're born and raised at. The other parish president always stepped up with our roofs. But this one here, he wants to neglect us. Why, I don't know."

In reality, the neglect comes from higher up. In a desperate attempt to save southern Louisiana from the double whammy of rising seas and sinking land, the Army Corps of Engineers has planned a billion-dollar, seventy-two-mile system of levees called the Morganza to the Gulf of Mexico Hurricane Protection Project. Instead of running alongside rivers, these levees will be more like the dikes in the Netherlands: Everything inside the wall will be protected by the Corps; everything outside will be sacrificed to the sea. Extending the wall to include Isle de Jean Charles would cost about one hundred million dollars. "We did originally try to put them in there," Jerome Zeringue, director of the Terrebonne Levee and Conservation District, told the *New York Times*. "The problem is, based on the cost-benefit ratio, it would cost too much to include that sliver of land. For the cost, you could buy the island and all the residents tenfold."

Maybe he meant residences? In any case, the Corps' triage determined that Isle de Jean Charles could not be saved. It's the type of plight that we think doesn't happen in America. But in the Mississippi River Delta, it's been going on for years.

And now the spill. Kadoo said he'd trade the oil spill for a storm any day. "We been through storms. You know when you got a storm comin', and you know you gotta get outta here. You know you gonna be out for a couple of weeks. And you know they gonna shut down the oysters for maybe two months at the most, and then you know you can go back to work. Here, we don't have no idea. Dis a blind shot. Everybody's been affected.

Shrimpers are catching hell. Crab fishermen. Everybody's catching hell. BP can't support us. They can give us so much money, but they can't support us. I got a lawyer. You never know what's gonna happen."

For at least 180 years the Biloxi-Chitimacha Indians, an offshoot of the Choctaw, have made their living from the fish, shrimp, and oysters in the waters around Isle de Jean Charles. They used to farm, too, but now the island soil is so saline that little will grow. Some of their former cornfields are now completely underwater. "We raised crops, we had wells," one member of the neighboring Pointe-au-Chien tribe told the local paper. "We can't anymore because of the salt water intrusion." Today fishing makes up three quarters of locals' income.

The first person known to inhabit the island was Jean Marie Naquin around 1828. His child, Jean Baptiste Narcisse Naquin, was born there in 1841 and became the first chief of the island community. The settlers built houses from mud and moss, a technique known as "bousillage," and covered them with palmetto thatch roofs. Wooden houses didn't arrive until the 1900s. While the islanders are proud of their Indian heritage, they are essentially part of the great mixing pot of bayou culture, spiced liberally with French names and ancestry.

Isle de Jean Charles is simply the highest ridge along the natural levees—the raised riverbanks—of Bayou St. Jean Charles, a minor bayou that curls down from Houma a few miles east of Dulac and Bayou Grand Caillou. Long ago, the levees of Bayou St. Jean Charles were probably dry all the way to where it merges with Bayou Terrebonne, but they have long since sunk beneath the saltwater. Isle de Jean Charles is the last remaining habitable spot—depending on how you define "habitable." The flooded bayou runs through the middle of the island. Now it is simply a channel connecting open water on both ends. Twisted, precarious wooden boardwalks cross from the road to the collapsing houses.

The island community was quite isolated, traveling the three to four miles to the "mainland" of Pointe-aux-Chenes—the town at the tip of the nearest bayou—in hand-poled skiffs called pirogues, until the island road was constructed in 1953. That was the heyday for Isle de Jean Charles. More than two hundred people lived on the island. There was a school, a fire station, a grocery store, a church, a dance hall. That's all gone now. A few dozen families, all sharing a handful of last names, remain on the island. Half the homes are abandoned. The cemetery hasn't been used since the 1940s. The most notable thing on the island is some sort of bathysphere built a few years ago for a B horror movie set in the swamps.

Isle de Jean Charles is falling to pieces. That's no metaphor. It is slowly sinking, eroding as it goes. The marshes around it, too, are dying and disintegrating. Being one of the most isolated and exposed communities in the delta, Isle de Jean Charles is showing some of the most acute signs of this delta rot, but the condition is chronic throughout the Barataria-Terrebonne Estuary. "It's the fastest-disappearing land mass on Earth," said Kerry St. Pé, a marine biologist who is director of the Barataria-Terrebonne National Estuary Program. And that adds a deep irony to the cleanup efforts here. Twenty-four square miles of Louisiana erodes and vanishes every year. Even if we manage to remove every drop of oil from the 580 miles of greased coastline without harming a single bird or blade of grass, southern Louisiana will still have sunk beneath the saltwater in fifty years. Levees will not save it. Raising houses on stilts will not save it. We are defending a dead land walking. It is the United States' most pressing environmental calamity. Yet, amazingly, although everybody in bayou country is all too familiar with the problem, the urgency hasn't registered with the rest of the country. As a rule, the canals of the oil industry get about half the blame for the situation, the river modifications of the Army Corps of Engineers the other half. But knowing what went wrong does not mean that anybody has any realistic idea what can be done to fix it.

At least nine thousand miles of canals riddle the bayou like termite tunnels, steadily dug by the oil industry since the 1930s, when geologists first realized that the marshes were full of oil and natural gas deposits. Until recently, the method for finding those deposits was simplistic. Floating dredges would dig a canal straight through a virgin area. Behind them would come an exploratory rig, inching along like a giant tick, punching holes blindly until it hit a reservoir. About 90 percent of the holes came up dry, meaning the number of holes punctuating the delta is mind-boggling. This exploration left a network of "keyhole canals," where the dredge would cut the canal, make a loop at the end, and come back. They look just like cul-de-sacs in a subdivision, only the houses are missing. When oil or gas was found, underwater pipelines (requiring their own canals) were laid to carry the goods to refineries. Like some sort of cyborg, the marshes now have a metal framework beneath their living surface.

You may wonder why the American Indian tribes of the bayou gave the oil companies permission to do this. The answer is that they had no say in the matter. (As the oil tycoon J. Paul Getty infamously said, "the meek shall inherit the earth, but not the mineral rights.") After the Louisiana Purchase in 1803, the federal government controlled southern Louisiana. It honored some legitimate land claims, if they could be proved, but Louisiana's Indian tribes were wholly illiterate and probably never even aware of the wheeling and dealing going on in New Orleans courthouses. The feds quickly sold the land to speculators, who in turn sold it to oil companies in the twentieth century. The tribes have launched some lawsuits to regain their lands, but since they have never been recognized by the government as sovereign tribes, they have little legal standing.

And less and less ground to stand on, legal or otherwise. Those nine thousand miles of canals form an alternate water transportation system that acts very differently than the natural bayous, which, as distributaries of the Mississippi River, were fresh and had a general direction of flow: out toward the Gulf of Mexico. True, they flowed very slowly, except during floods, and were tidal along their lower reaches—saltwater would encroach every high tide—but their upper reaches stayed fresh. The marshes acted like a skin or permeable membrane for the delta, allowing freshwater to flush the region with nutrients before exiting to the Gulf, but preventing deadly saltwater from penetrating too far into the living marsh. Strong salinity occurred only where the outer fringe of the marshes bordered the Gulf of Mexico, with brackish areas intruding a little farther inland.

Not being connected to a river system, the oil canals don't work that way. Instead, they are simply ideal conduits for the salty Gulf of Mexico, allowing it to infiltrate virtually every nook of the marshes. There are, broadly, two types of marshes on the Gulf Coast. Salt marshes, made of grasses that thrive in saline conditions, skirt the perimeter. Behind them are the freshwater marshes. These don't mind a brackish intrusion, having evolved to survive the encroachment of saltwater during the dry fall and winter, as well as the occasional salty dose of a hurricane, but they die if their roots are constantly exposed to salt.

Which is exactly what is happening along every bank of every canal. As the exposed grasses die, their roots decay. Those roots are the only thing holding the muddy soil in place, so the soil collapses into the waves churned up by the next storm, and then the cycle is repeated with the next rank of grasses. This is why the Houma Navigation Canal has expanded from 250 feet to 800 feet in fifty years. Eventually, the saltwater reaches beyond the marshes to the next ecosystem, the cypress swamps. That is what killed the cypress swamp Wendy Billiot showed me. And the Houma Nav's destructiveness is dwarfed by New Orleans's infamous Mississippi River–Gulf Outlet Canal, known as "MR. GO," built in the 1960s to give ships a direct route from the Gulf to New Orleans, which quickly killed thirty-nine thousand acres of cypress swamp, transforming it into dead trunks and salt marsh.

Bill Finch had explained to me how freakish a sight that is. "You'll never see a salt marsh next to a bald cypress community unless something's gone wrong. In Louisiana, it's gone wrong. The marsh is retreating so fast that it's being slammed into these cypress, and they're dying, and you're capturing that snapshot."

The same thing is occurring throughout the delta. Almost *half* of Plaquemines Parish, which straddles the lower Mississippi, has been destroyed by subsidence and saltwater intrusion, with Lafourche and Terrebonne parishes not far behind.

Until the 1980s, the oil industry was never required to backfill the canals it dug (nor to stop dumping billions of gallons of toxic brine brought up from oil wells into thousands of waste pits throughout the marshes). Even today, it only backfills canals once it officially abandons them—which it has little incentive to do. In 2005, the Louisiana Supreme Court ruled that oil companies couldn't be forced to backfill old canals unless the original contract required them to do so—and virtually none of the old contracts did. Meanwhile, the spoil banks that line the canals (had to put the mud somewhere!) further block the natural flow of water through the delta, playing havoc with the hydrology. Spoil banks can be spotted from miles away by the presence of invasive Chinese tallow trees (known locally as chicken trees or popcorn trees), which proliferate on the relatively dry raised land of the spoil banks.

As if the canals weren't enough, the oil industry has been undermining the marshes in a second way, this one literal. You'd think anyone standing atop miles of soft sediment and porous rock would hesitate before pumping out the gas and oil filling the spaces in the rock, but nobody did. Areas from which oil and gas are removed subside two to three times faster than other areas. Today companies continue to pump natural gas out of the marshes, with predictable results: Many places sink a half inch per year as the ground beneath them deflates. And as they sink, the saltwater rushes in that much higher.

So the residents of the delta, human and otherwise, can thank the oil industry for the loss of at least one thousand square miles—640,000 acres—of marshland. An equal amount of blame gets placed at the feet of the Army Corps of Engineers and its two-hundred-year battle with the Mississippi River.

To the Corps' credit, it must be said that it was only doing what it had been asked to do. Until the eighteenth century, the Mississippi River flooded almost every year, leaving the land wet for months on end and caked in a fresh inch of mud. This sucks if you have built a house in the lowlands or if you are trying to grow crops—two things the first American Indians were never foolish enough to try. They had a supremely logical way to deal with the rich but low-lying area: They came, they fished, and they left.

But the first European settlers in the area had big ideas. The size and navigability of the Mississippi River made it immensely important. In those pre-highway days, it offered the only access to half a continent of fertile floodplain—and growing populations. The French staked out New Orleans in the early 1700s to control the river's access, founding the "Crescent City" on the closest thing to high ground they could find—the natural levees, or raised banks, that had formed along a crescent-shaped bend in the river. Even that area flooded on occasion, so the settlers artificially raised the levees with three feet of earth. That helped, though all it really did was push all that water to the other side of the river, much to the consternation of the farmers there. Soon they had erected levees of their own—which simply held that water back just long enough to flood their downstream neighbors, who soon wanted levees of their own.

The pattern was set. As new levees kept the floodplains dry, more and more river plantations prospered. Whenever some new flood wiped them out, they'd improve their levees, forcing that much more floodwater onto the land of anyone who hadn't done the same. The farmers also drained the swamps, the better to raise sugarcane and other crops. Since these porous swamps had functioned like surgical sponges, soaking up the bleeding from the Mississippi's main artery, that left less and less area to absorb floodwaters.

By the end of the eighteenth century, the levee arms race had achieved a kind of détente. The river from Baton Rouge down was fully leveed, the only major outlets being the bayous that peeled off from the main river, which now received far more water during floods than ever before.

New Orleans had by then become a major trading port, sending Midwestern and Southern goods to the world in exchange for rum, tobacco, and slaves to work the plantations. It was seedy and cosmopolitan, the Mos Eisley spaceport of its day. Pirates, traders, smugglers, entrepreneurs, and waves of money came and went with the tides. In 1762 Spain seized control, and in 1798 it closed the port to Americans upriver, before finally turning ownership back over to Napoléon in 1801. The young American state understood that the Mississippi River was the lifeblood of its western territories, so in 1803 President Thomas Jefferson dispatched James Monroe and Robert Livingston to Paris to negotiate port access. They were prepared to offer ten million dollars.

As serendipity would have it, at that moment Napoléon found himself in a bind. His European war was sapping France's resources from other spots. He had already lost Haiti and was losing his grip throughout the Caribbean. Napoléon was pretty sure he couldn't hold Louisiana against the British, who were on the rise in the Gulf of Mexico. He sure as hell didn't want it to fall into their hands. Plus he desperately needed funds to continue his war. So when Monroe and Livingston showed up to try to buy access to New Orleans, Napoléon's representative beat them to the punch and said, How about fifteen million dollars for the whole thing? By "whole thing," he meant all of Louisiana, and why not take Oklahoma, Arkansas, Missouri, Iowa, Kansas, Nebraska, the Dakotas, and parts of Minnesota, New Mexico, Colorado, Wyoming, and Montana as a bonus?

Thomas Jefferson said okay.

In the annals of sweetheart deals, this ranks up there with the

Yankees buying Babe Ruth from the Red Sox in 1919. Napoléon's excuse was that the enemy of his enemy was his friend. "This accession of territory affirms forever the power of the United States," he said after the Louisiana Purchase went through, "and I have given England a maritime rival who sooner or later will humble her pride." In this sense, it was more like if the Red Sox had sold Babe Ruth to the Detroit Tigers.

In any case, Napoléon was right. During the War of 1812 America did humble England's pride, at least in New Orleans, where Andrew Jackson routed the British and jump-started his own strange career. But the Americans believed the British would be back, so Congress dispatched a team from the Army Corps of Engineers to New Orleans to fortify the city, improve the levee system, and keep the river navigable. The Corps has been on the job ever since.

Throughout the nineteenth century, the Corps continued to dam bayous, "saving" residents of each waterway from flooding. In doing so, it also choked the bayous, turning them from lazy rivers into stagnant canals open only to the Gulf. It responded to increasingly worse floods by raising, expanding, and extending the existing levees. In Louisiana, some of the levees grew twelve feet high and a hundred feet wide.

If you have a hose with four leaks and you plug three, you know what happens: The fourth hole spurts all the harder. This is what happened on the Mississippi, and it was not lost on the engineers of the Corps, who became convinced that the only way to truly control the river was to give it no outlet, to expose no point of weakness. Keeping all the water in the main channel, they believed, would also keep the river bottom from silting up, an ongoing problem. (Today, the Corps dredges the river continuously to maintain a shipping channel forty-five feet deep from the mouth of the river to Baton Rouge and nine feet deep from Baton Rouge all the way to Minneapolis.) By the turn of the century, the river was shackled for two thousand miles, all the way to the Gulf, where it blasted its contents with unnatural force into the abyss.

The river was also much higher than it had ever been. When water levels were low and the river was slow, sediment continued to drop out onto the riverbed, raising the height of the bed and the average height of the river. When water levels were high, all that water that would have normally found its way into the end-less creeks, bayous, swamps, and marshes of the delta was now constrained within the main river channel, climbing on top of itself like a crowd trying to escape a runaway train through a single door in the caboose. The river surged eight, ten, fifteen feet above the surrounding countryside, a liquid monorail.

Meanwhile, the land around it was subsiding. Occasional floods blew out the levees, wrecked crops, drowned farmers and livestock, and deposited several years' worth of sediment in one muddy mess. But the response by the Corps each time was to build the levees—which themselves were sinking—higher, wider, stronger. Floods became less frequent, though far more cata-strophic. Mostly, the water and all its sediment headed for the Gulf, and the lands of the bayous, denied new infusions, contin-ued to die. Of the six thousand square miles of wetland that the Mississippi has managed to create since the last ice age, nearly two thousand have been lost so far. That's two thousand square miles of fish nurseries, shrimping grounds, storm buffers, recre-ational paradise, and homes.

Though anecdotal reports of something amiss—oystermen in Breton Sound complaining that their oyster reefs had died from increased salinity; building foundations slipping below sea level—trickled in through the early twentieth century, the idea that all of southern Louisiana could be sinking was so extreme that no one took it seriously. The Great Flood of 1927 blew apart levees throughout the river's length and killed more than a thousand people. The Corps' response was reflexive: bigger levees. Many grew thirty feet high. The only part of southern Louisiana still receiving its annual topping of sediment was the delta of the Atchafalaya River, the Mississippi's most important distributary and, once its connection to Bayou Lafourche was closed in 1904, its only one. The Atchafalaya, which departs the Mississippi 315 miles upstream and takes 30 percent of the water with it, has been left to meander on its 147-mile journey to the Gulf, so it continues to build land today. (If left to its own devices, it would be building *a lot* of land, because the Mississippi has been trying to switch its main channel to the Atchafalaya for the past century. This would leave Baton Rouge, New Orleans, and the American oil and petrochemical industries high and dry; relocating a hundred miles of factories, employees, and transportation infrastructure to what is currently a swamp is not realistic, nor is waiting out the river's decades-long shifting process. Thus, since the 1950s, the Army Corps of Engineers has been waging a very uncertain battle to prevent this change.)

Not until the 1970s did the technology arrive to back up the anecdotal mutterings with some hard science. A Louisiana State University scientist named Woody Gagliano compared old and new aerial photos with topographical maps and determined that the state was losing land—*a lot* of land. Gagliano sounded the alarm, but the powers that be didn't listen to this inconvenient truth. What were they going to do? Divert the Mississippi?

Well, yes. They needed to build freshwater diversions into the river levees. A diversion is a fancy name for what is basically a concrete gate, looking kind of like an underpass, through which a tiny portion of the Mississippi is channeled out of the main stem and into a basin that serves as a sediment trap, collecting the dirt that builds new wetlands. Part of Ol' Muddy had to be sent through the marshes to unload its mud before it reached the Gulf. That was the only solution. And an insanely expensive solution it would be. Woody Gagliano kept banging the drum, but it was twenty years before the first freshwater diversion was built on the Mississippi—and that was created not to build land but to save oysters. The 1991 Caernarvon Freshwater Diversion sent a few thousand cubic feet of water per second through five fifteen-foot gated culverts eighty-one miles upriver into the fabled oyster grounds of Breton Sound, on the east side of the river. It was just a trickle, but it immediately began improving oyster habitat by reducing the salinity of the water—and building land as a side effect. It worked. Oysters proliferated. Ducks, largemouth bass, muskrats, and alligators returned. Brown shrimp, blue crabs, and redfish exited. The area, which had been losing a thousand acres of marsh per year, rebuilt thousands of new acres over the next decade.

By the time Caernarvon was built, the Corps had realized its error, but its options were as constrained as the river's. Over the second half of the twentieth century, several million people had begun living and farming on the floodplains of southern Louisiana, protected by the levees. The bulk of the petrochemical industry, attracted by the world-class shipping access and waste disposal offered by the river, had taken up residence along the banks of the Mississippi between Baton Rouge and New Orleans. Eliminating the levees and letting the river flow freely was not an option.

Today, the Mississippi River is the highest natural feature in bayou country. But you can't see it. You drive for hours, stealing glances at your map, knowing that the great river must be right around here somewhere, and thinking that surely you would see it if it weren't for that colossal grassy embankment skirting the road. Only when you eventually climb the embankment to a bridge—or note the antennae of a supertanker gliding silently along the other side, high in the air—do you sheepishly realize that the embankment is no landfill, and that it has been preventing countless billions of gallons of water from obliterating your car and all the surrounding countryside. Like a stupendously rich capitalist, the Mississippi can be both generously philanthropic and unpredictably destructive.

To reawaken the river's philanthropic side, the Corps and its governmental and nonprofit partners have spent the past twenty years creating a number of diversions on the river. Since its enactment in 1990, the Coastal Wetlands Planning, Protection and Restoration Act—known as the Breaux Act, for its main sponsor, Louisiana senator John Breaux—has "diverted" about forty million dollars of federal money annually toward coastal restoration. Certain projects have gone better than others. At first, some of the land built consisted of little more than multi-acre, solid masses of mud, but what most wetland creatures need is that magical edge where grass and water meet. Juvenile shrimp, you'll recall, live in the edges of marshes, hiding and feeding amid the submerged bases of the grasses. They can't travel over land. What matters for them and most other marsh denizens is the total amount of linear edge, not the total acreage. And that edge is crumbling.

Half of Louisiana's shrimp harvest occurs in the salt marshes. One hundred percent of Louisiana's shrimp live in the marshes during part of their lives. Since shrimp like saltwater, they have fared better than oysters, which prefer it brackish, and they've kept moving farther into the marshes, following the salinity. But their available habitat—their potential food supply—is a fraction of what it once was. "The land being gone the way it is, it makes our season shorter," shrimper Ricky Polkey told the *New York Times*. "The shrimp size has been very small because they don't have a place to hide, where they would hole up and grow in the marshes before going out to the gulf. It seems we work all year for less than a dollar a pound."

More recent diversion projects have become much better at creating marshes that mimic natural ones, but the amount of land creation from these projects has barely put a dent in the rate of land loss. Creating an area the size of Manhattan—the amount of land being lost annually—and doing it carefully, every year, so that it actually makes good habitat, is ungodly expensive. All the governmental agencies and nonprofit groups in the country have struggled to collectively raise more than a few hundred million dollars a year for coastal restoration, while current estimates for truly restoring the Gulf Coast start at a hundred billion dollars. Most sober observers have made the understandable conclusion that there's no way in hell such a huge sum of money will become available, and, while continuing to call for a national response to Gulf restoration, in their minds they have quietly begun to write off the wetlands.

I visited Kadoo again two months later. His life had changed dramatically. All the oyster grounds were still closed to fishing, and rumors abounded that they might be closed for years. If you think this would have demoralized Kadoo, think again. He was ebullient. BP had stationed one of its spill-response headquarters at Pointe-aux-Chenes after the tribe had asked for boom to

protect its marshes from the reddish-orange glops of oil creeping into them, and had hired Kadoo to patrol the marshes for oil
and tend the boom. "I love it!" he told me when I met him at six
in the morning to head out. "Best job I ever had! I'm through
wit oysters!" It was better money than he made oystering, physically unchallenging, a chance to rip across the water in a shiny
new skiff at thirty miles per hour, plus he got a hot breakfast and
bag lunch every day. Best of all, he felt respected.

As Kadoo outfitted me in requisite hard hat, safety glasses,
orange vest, and steel-toe boots, and we met up with Chatt
Smith, BP's base manager for Pointe-aux-Chenes, I realized
how essential the locals had become. The area is changing so fast
that the maps are virtually useless. When we left the dock, we
boated beneath power lines that had been on dry ground thirty
years ago. Now they were sunk so deep, their poles cocked at
alarming angles, that the boat channel ducked right through
them. "Pointe-aux-Chenes" means "Oak Point." We passed a
forest of dead oak trees sticking out of the water, their skeletal
trunks bleached by the sun. I asked Kadoo if he remembered
them. "Oh, sure," he said. "Them trees was alive fifteen years
ago." Eventually the oak stumps will rot and fall, and the name
of the place will seem nonsensical to future visitors. Locals who
have moved away and come back to visit are left speechless. The
places of their childhood have not simply changed; they have
ceased to exist.

As a ripe, red sun climbed over the grasses and pushed into a
stew of storm clouds, we slalomed through the marsh channels,
hands clamped on top of our hard hats. The artificial breeze felt
great, keeping the humid air at bay. In the limitless distance, the
marsh grass—a glowing green where it emerged from the water,
fading to a parched beige at the tips—could have been fields of

wheat, rippling in the wind. We could see bands of rain miles away. When they hit, the drops lashed our cheeks like shrapnel. Every now and then we passed a sign emerging from the water saying WARNING: PETROLEUM PIPELINE. DO NOT ANCHOR OR DREDGE—a first hint of the trouble beneath the surface of this place. Thousands of miles of pipelines snake through the wetlands, about four feet underwater. Every now and then a boat hits a pipeline or a wellhead and natural gas spews into the air, a miniature *Deepwater Horizon*.

(One of the many hidden ways that oil money powers Louisiana is that oil companies must pay oyster-ground leaseholders every time they need to cross the underwater leases to access their wellheads or to service pipelines. Many leaseholders make more in access fees than they do selling oysters.)

In the rush to protect these marshes in the days after the explosion, teams had placed white absorbent cotton boom in front of them, because that was all they had. But cotton boom quickly gets fouled with all sorts of mud and algae, so now the spill-response team was bringing in heavy-duty yellow plastic boom, fighting petroleum with more petroleum products. Barges piled high with shrink-wrapped palettes of yellow boom were stationed in central areas. Two-man crews in skiffs were loading their boats with the new yellow boom and returning soiled, white cotton boom to the barges. It would eventually wind up in some Gulf Coast landfill.

Around one bend in the marsh, we came upon two tubby, bearded biker types leaning over the side of their skiff and yanking furiously on a stuck boom anchor. "Y'all are never gonna get that," said Chatt. He radioed for a larger boat with a winch. We followed a liquid labyrinth through the grasses. "I don't know how you can find your way through this," I told Kadoo. He smiled and shrugged. With the sun higher, I could see dead oaks rising out of the marsh grass in the foreground and the towers of oil and gas facilities in the distance.

A flock of about fifty white pelicans, huge and pink-billed, stood on a shoal at the edge of the marsh. "They always right there," said Kadoo. "That's home." Chatt radioed headquarters to make sure somebody came out and boomed the pelicans' home.

Eventually we emerged into a wide bay. We could see a dozen spill-response skiffs searching for oil and collecting boom from barges. On the map, this spot was called Lake Tambour. From there, we traveled to Lake Barre, then Lake Felicity. But all this time we were simply boating through open water. Chatt explained that when the chart was made, thirty years earlier, each "lake" was bounded by treed shorelines. Now those shores were gone. No wonder BP needed local watermen like Kadoo to navigate the area.

I asked Kadoo if the population of Isle de Jean Charles was going down. "It ain't comin' up," he said. "We lose a few more every hurricane."

"You know you're going to have to leave someday," Chatt said gently.

"When I die."

This tenacious attitude has served the bayou people well for generations, allowing them to tough it out through endless hardships. "We're a resilient people," they say. Then again, I'm still waiting for the group that, when faced with natural disaster, says, "We're not particularly resilient. When the going gets tough, we pretty much pack it in and move on." I think I'd sign on with that group. Before Hurricanes Katrina and Rita, before Gustav, before the oil spill, the federal government had spent $439,000 per resident to protect the town of Grand Isle from storms. Now that figure probably tops $1 million per resident—with nothing to show for it. Like a porcupine holding its ground against an onrushing automobile, the "never retreat" attitude may be suicidal this time. People sometimes hold up Isle de Jean Charles as the first casualty of the wetlands debacle, but that just goes to show how short our memories are, how quickly we readjust to the dire status quo, like the proverbial frogs in the cooking pot. You don't hear about communities such as Sea Breeze and Manila Village anymore—communities that also raised themselves on stilts to survive—because they no longer exist. They were a bit farther out toward the Gulf, a teensy bit lower in elevation than Isle de Jean Charles. And they are gone. Wiped off the face of the earth and the memories of all but the oldest of old-timers.

Among the places worst hit by the oil spill were a chain of barrier islands off the coast of Terrebonne Parish. Raccoon Island, Whiskey Island, Trinity Island, and East Island were the site of intense cleanup efforts, including some of Governor Bobby Jindal's loopy plans to create a berm of protection by dredging sand out of the sea. These scrawny islands, considered important bird habitat but uninhabitable, are all that remain of a place once known as Isle Dernière. In the 1850s, Isle Dernière boasted one hundred homes, several hotels, and more than a few gambling establishments. It was considered Louisiana's premier resort, the Grand Isle of its day. And it no longer exists, done in first by an 1856 hurricane, which killed half of the four hundred people on the island at the time, and then by subsidence ever since. One of the most shocking moments in my Gulf Coast education was when I first saw maps of Isle Dernière in 1853 and its remnants today. The beach—gone. The thousands of acres of marsh that it sheltered—all open water now.

Which is why I found that boat ride through the Barataria-Terrebonne Estuary so surreal. I could see how hard and earnestly BP's whole team was working. There were 250 people at Pointe-aux-Chenes, more than half of them local tribe members, and 140 of the workers were on the water tending boom and patrolling for oil. They'd clocked 144,000 man-hours by July. And all to save a sinking land. BP wasn't just rearranging the deck chairs on the *Titanic*; it was scrubbing them clean with soap.

I'm sure Kadoo wasn't thinking about all this as we tore through Terrebonne Bay, checking on the miles of orange and yellow plastic that now skirted the sinking marshes. He was living for the moment—an admirable quality. Still, watching all the places of his childhood vanish over the past fifty years, he must have allowed it to sink in subconsciously, must have quietly stewed on the implications. Because when I asked him what he planned to do once this job was over, he said, "Stick with this spill-response stuff. I got my training. Always be a spill somewhere."

Chapter 9

TEN THOUSAND CUTS

To me, the most chilling article published during the summer of 2010 was not about oil-eating bacteria, petroleum-smeared pelicans, or exploding rigs. It was not about BP at all. It was not even about Louisiana's crumbling marshes. To me, the piece that made me sit back from my laptop and shiver was an unassuming little snippet published in the July 29 issue of *Nature* titled "Global Phytoplankton Decline over the Past Century." In the article, a team from Canada's Dalhousie University shows that the planet's phytoplankton populations have been declining about 1 percent per year, leading to a 40 percent reduction in phytoplankton since 1950.

That should have caused massive riots all over the world, and emergency summits of global leaders, because if phytoplankton continue to decline at that pace, we can all just pack it in. Phytoplankton feed almost all the fish on Earth. They produce half the oxygen and sequester as much carbon dioxide as all the forests on the planet. If phytoplankton are truly declining, then the oceans are dying, and the rest of us are, too. We cannot survive without the seas.

I bring this up not because I have any solutions, and not because I want to ruin your day, but simply because I want to put the BP spill in perspective and point out an irony. After the accident, people who never gave a damn about the Redneck Riviera became suddenly tearful with concern for the Gulf's wildlife and human communities. They were also convinced that 205 million gallons of oil, plus a couple of million gallons of dispersant, would kill off all the life in the Gulf in a black cloud of toxic waste. But the truth is that we have been screwing the Gulf for decades.

"Same ole same ole," Diane Wilson, a fourth-generation Texas shrimper turned environmental activist, wrote on Grist. "I hate to say it, but what I'm seeing now in the Gulf ain't nothing new. The toxic releases, the lies, the cover-ups, the skimping on safety, the nonexistent documents, the 'swinging door' with regulators, the deaths . . . This is the biggest flame among the thousands of fires set by Corporate America on its Sherman-like march across the Gulf."

Some of those flames are literal. One of the most enduring images of the BP fiasco is the gigantic pilot light atop the drill ship *Discover Enterprise* as it siphoned petroleum from the blown-out well. That petroleum was a mix of oil and natural gas. The liquid oil can be captured, but the lighter natural gas can't. It had to be flared off to prevent any risk of explosion. (It was natural gas that blew up the *Deepwater Horizon* in the first place.)

Crude is always a mix of oils and natural gases. Ideally, the gases are captured and sent through pipelines to refineries. Sometimes they can be reinjected into the ground. But often, the technology isn't in place, and the only safe way to deal with the gas is to flare it.

"Safe" being a relative term. Flaring may prevent explosions, but it also releases tons of volatile organic compounds (VOCs) into the atmosphere. Benzene, toluene, arsenic, mercury—all the usual suspects.

Even the gases that get sent to refineries sometimes have to be flared. All need to be cooked. Refineries are basically toxic chemical plants, and the Gulf Coast has the highest concentration of refineries in the country, for the very good reason that more crude (both domestic and international) arrives at Gulf ports than anywhere else. A refinery is a giant still. Crude is a bouillabaisse of hundreds of different hydrocarbons, along with small amounts of other chemicals. All hydrocarbons are made of hydrogen and carbon, but the bigger and heavier the molecular chain, the thicker the product. Methane, the simplest hydrocarbon, has just one carbon atom, surrounded by four hydrogen atoms. Propane has three to four carbons and is also a gas at normal temperatures. Gasoline has seven to nine. Diesel has eleven to eighteen and is notoriously thick at cold temperatures. Fuel oil has twenty to twenty-seven carbons. Asphalt has more than thirty-five and is more solid than liquid. Since all these hydrocarbons boil at different temperatures, they have different uses and need to be separated. A refinery boils crude, sending the different products into different receptacles, just as is done in a still with alcohol and water.

Seen from a distance, a typical refinery looks a bit like a NASA space center. A forest of cylinders points skyward, but they aren't rockets. They are boilers, distillation units, storage tanks, and exhaust pipes, connected by miles of metal piping. When somebody needs an image of industrial hell, of *Road Warrior* landscapes, an image of a refinery is often used. They are noisy, smelly, foul, dangerous places. Release of atmospheric pollution is part and parcel of what they do. Refineries produce numerous VOCs associated with cancer, breathing problems, and birth defects. Of the many refinery VOCs, benzene is the most notorious. If you live within thirty miles of a refinery, you're probably being exposed to dangerous levels of benzene.

Since the business of refineries is to bring highly flammable material to extremely high temperatures, it's no wonder they are dangerous places to work. Before the Macondo well blowout forever linked BP to the term "oil spill," the corporation was best known for its Texas City refinery disaster of 2005. An explosion of flammable gas killed 15 people and injured 180. As in the *Deepwater Horizon* disaster, cost-cutting shortcuts and inadequate maintenance were blamed. (BP eventually paid out more than $2 billion in damage claims.)

Explosions, leaks, and toxic chemical releases are regular occurrences at refineries. (Which helps explain why most Gulf states rank near the top in toxic releases, though other chemical industries certainly contribute their fair share.) Chevron's Richmond, California, refinery released nearly twenty-five thousand pounds of carcinogens in 2001 alone. It produces more than two million pounds of waste each year *when things are going right.* Chevron's even larger Pascagoula Refinery, which perches right on the edge of Mississippi Sound, suffered a major fire in 2007 that sent toxic soot into the countryside. The thousand-acre refinery processes fourteen million gallons of crude per day into gasoline, jet fuel, diesel, propane, petroleum coke, sulfur, paraxylene, benzene, and ethylbenzene.

This is the nature of refineries. It can't be helped—not if we all want to keep our homes warm and our cars rolling. Laws require all new refineries to do a better job of cleaning their emissions, but existing refineries were grandfathered into the system. (The industry argued that it couldn't afford to upgrade.) This is part of the reason no major new refinery has been built in the United States in the past thirty-five years.

The collateral damage from oil industry activity doesn't end there. There is the case of "produced water." When drilling rigs first puncture a new oil or gas reservoir, the pressure inside the reservoir forces the oil and gas to the surface all on its own—as happened on the *Deepwater Horizon*. There is usually some small amount of water in the mix at first. After that petroleum has shot out of the well for a while, however, pressure drops. To keep the petroleum shooting to the surface, rigs inject water into the reservoir, filling the space and increasing the pressure, forcing oil out. Initially, what comes up the well is mostly petroleum; but later, the percentage of produced water increases. Toward the end of a well's life, most of its contents will be produced water.

Drillers need to do something with this huge volume of water—which isn't merely water, of course. Because it has mixed with the contents of the reservoir, produced water is full of toxic chemicals and radioactive compounds, including benzene, toluene, mercury, and radium. It's nasty stuff. In the early days of the industry, it was simply dumped in open evaporation pits. By the 1970s, companies couldn't get away with that anymore, so they began injecting it underground—except in places without strong environmental watchdog organizations. In Ecuador, Texaco dumped 18 *billion* gallons of produced water, along with a 16-million-gallon oil chaser, into the rivers of the rainforest, according to the Amazon Defense Coalition, which is suing Chevron, Texaco's parent. Texaco's own audit, commissioned in 1990 as the company was skulking out of Ecuador, and revealed in court in August 2010, left the prosecution little to do. "All twenty-two production stations are currently, or have at some time, discharged oily produced water to the environment and flared excess gas," the audit stated. It identified "hydrocarbon contamination requiring remediation at all production facilities and a majority of the drill sites . . . Produced water (which contains carcinogens and toxic heavy metals) is being discharged to the environment in all cases . . . Produced waste is then passed through a series of open, unlined pits. The remaining oil emulsion and produced water is discharged into a local creek or river or in some instances directly into the jungle."

Could never happen in the United States, of course—except in places without strong environmental watchdog organizations. As Kierán Suckling, founder of the Center for Biological Diversity, explained, "the environmental movement was either so far removed from [the Gulf] that it was unaware, or it was aware and afraid to challenge it because of local politics. Or it was unwilling to challenge because it has written off the Gulf as America's dumping ground." Indeed, in the 1990s companies were still illegally dumping produced water along the Gulf Coast. Even today offshore rigs are allowed to dump millions of pounds of produced water into the Gulf.

If you think the states are going to stop them, think again. New Orleans's *Times-Picayune* examined Louisiana's coastal-zone permitting program and found that in the past five years, 4,500 permits had been issued to the oil industry to operate along the coast; not a single application had been denied. Not surprising when an impressive chunk of the state's revenues and campaign contributions come from the petroleum industry.

Rigs are also allowed to dump drilling mud, a far more noxious material. A decade ago, while Bill Finch was working as a reporter for the *Mobile Press-Register*, he and Ben Raines analyzed tests of fish and shrimp caught near rigs and found that they had far higher mercury levels—up to twenty-five times more—than those caught far away from rigs. That pattern held for the sediment around the rigs, which is also much higher in mercury than normal sediment—undoubtedly because the rigs are allowed to dump their drilling fluids into the Gulf, so long as those fluids contain less than 1 part per million mercury. (The EPA originally sought a zero-mercury rule, but the industry successfully argued that this would be too costly.) "I've seen tanker trucks dump two hundred loads into a marsh outside of Seadrift, Texas," Diane Wilson wrote. With more than one billion pounds of drilling fluids dumped annually, that still adds up to half a ton of mercury per year. Before the 1996 EPA regulations, barite, the primary component of drilling mud, could have up to 8 parts per million mercury, meaning that over the past half century hundreds of thousands of pounds of mercury have been dumped around the rigs. The sediment around many rigs is more contaminated than many Superfund sites closed because of mercury contamination.

This would be bad enough, but the real whammy is that the rigs are, as many fishermen I met on the Gulf Coast told me, the best place to fish. The four-thousand-plus rigs in the Gulf form the world's largest artificial reef system, an entirely new ecosystem that attracts reef fish such as snapper. Anglers across the coast head to the rigs to catch them. The impression is of abundant snapper populations, but in reality there are few breeding-age snappers anywhere else in the Gulf. Between the easy pickings beneath the reef and the millions of juvenile snapper killed in shrimp trawlers' nets, the breeding population of snappers in the Gulf has actually plunged by 97 percent since World War II.

And with so many of the ones around the rigs becoming somebody's dinner, the rigs have become mercury-delivery devices of the first order. Dumped drilling muds deposit mercury in the sediment, where bacteria ingest it. They are eaten by creatures such as marine worms, which are eaten by snapper, grouper, and other fish, which pass the mercury to the fishermen. When the *Press-Register* tested Gulf Coast residents who ate fish at least once a week, 80 percent had dangerously high mercury levels.

You get the picture. Even when things are good, the impact of the oil industry subtly degrades the entire Gulf region. Yet because most of this degradation happens at an incremental pace, and because so many of these effects are hard to measure, they never get added to the ledger when the industry is totaling up the costs and benefits of doing business. "The bottom line," said Diane Wilson, "is that the Gulf of Mexico dies a little every day from the tens of thousands of chemical plants, oil refineries, and oil and gas rigs that pockmark the Gulf and its coastlines. It's a death of ten thousand cuts, and many of these offenses don't get reported at all."

You already know about one of the biggest of those cuts—the canals dug through the wetlands by the industry's floating dredges. But other cuts often go unreported, such as the impact of the "air guns" used by the oil industry in its search for new reservoirs. These air guns are not pump-action Red Ryders in the hands of twelve-year-olds; they are underwater explosives that send waves of two-hundred-decibel noise energy tearing through the seas and bedrock and echoing back. Unfortunately, these explosions also permanently damage the ears of fish, cause lesions in the ears and brains of whales, trigger whale and dolphin strandings (as the disoriented animals try to get away from the painful sounds), bruise crabs' organs, and cause numerous changes of behavior in fish and cetaceans of all kinds. (They've also caused easily observable "changes of behavior" in divers unlucky enough to be caught near an air gun assault or a naval sonar operation.) Despite scientific consensus that human noise is having a severe effect on whales' ability to communicate and survive, no serious attempt to remedy the situation is in the works. (A recent National Resources Defense Council challenge to the U.S. Navy's sonar practices was laughed off by the Supreme Court in a 6–3 decision.)

Other cuts remain invisible, waiting to be felt. In light of the cement-plug failures that were partially responsible for the BP blowout, it is chilling to learn that there are currently 27,000 abandoned wells pricking the floor of the Gulf, most held back by nothing more than cement. Some of these wells date back to the original offshore rush of the 1940s. Their cement has been weathered by sixty-plus years of corrosive seawater. According to an Associated Press report, about 3,500 of these wells are "temporarily abandoned," meaning they were never capped permanently and have less-extensive cement plugs. Many of these wells were "temporarily abandoned" decades ago. Imagine the structural integrity of a cement building that's been sitting under the sea for many years; would you trust it to hold back a pressurized well? What about during hurricanes?

Oil companies are supposed to have one year to permanently seal a temporarily abandoned well. In reality, there has been virtually no oversight or incentive to comply, despite one estimate by the EPA that 17 percent of wells are improperly plugged and a 2001 report from the disgraced Minerals and Management Service indicating that many wells in the Gulf were already leaking.

In September 2010, two months after the AP story broke, the Obama administration issued a new order directing companies to permanently cap the 3,500 wells classified as temporarily abandoned, as well as to dismantle 650 of the 1,200 abandoned platforms in the Gulf. It remains to be seen whether this new directive has any more teeth.

In any case, the administration can't do a thing about all the active wells, or the thirty-three thousand miles of pipelines—enough to lap the earth and cross the Pacific a second time—that funnel oil and natural gas from offshore platforms and terminals to storage tanks and refineries. No matter how much of an emphasis the industry puts on safety, it can't keep control over such a vast infrastructure. Every hurricane that bowls through the Gulf causes problems. Every case of mechanical or human error has the potential to snowball. There have been more than three hundred offshore-drilling spills since the 1960s, and hundreds of accidents at U.S. refineries in the same time. The combined efforts of Hurricanes Katrina and Rita alone in 2005 spilled eleven million gallons of oil into the Gulf, a whole extra *Exxon Valdez*, as platforms toppled, pipelines broke, moorings snapped, anchors dragged, and tanks ruptured.

I hope I've convinced you that the oil industry has not been a good steward of the wetlands virtually handed to it a century ago. It should be on the hook—morally and, I hope, financially—for a lot of the damage. Yet the truth is that even if it had been a model citizen, we are perfectly capable of wrecking the Gulf of Mexico without its help. What's really killing the Gulf is the very thing that sustains it: the Mississippi River. And it has less to do with the oil industry than it has to do with all of us.

One of the most shocking statistics I learned throughout the twelve sad weeks of the Macondo well saga was this: At the height of the oil-response craziness, BP sprayed about 140,000 pounds of Corexit dispersant into the Gulf each day. Yet an equal amount of "dispersant"—the soaps and surfactants used in household detergents to break up grease—washes down the Mississippi into the Gulf every single day. People getting the bacon fat off their pans, automotive repair shops cleaning their bays, farmers mucking out their stalls, and the entire petrochemical industry use some of the same ingredients found in Corexit to keep America shiny. For example, the solvent 2-butoxyethanol, the most toxic ingredient in Corexit, is also what gives Windex and Simple Green that unforgettable smell. It's used in countless household products, from soaps and cosmetics to ink and paint, and it all finds its way down the Mississippi. For years, boaters in the Gulf have carried bottles of Dawn on board, ready to squirt it onto any accidental gas or oil spill to break it up. The irony reached an apotheosis worthy of Kafka when, after its planes had carpet-bombed the Gulf with the world's entire supply of Corexit, the Coast Guard delivered signs to Gulf Coast marinas that said WARNING: THE USE OF SOAPS OR OTHER DISPERSING AGENTS TO DISSIPATE OIL IS MORE HARMFUL TO THE MARINE ENVIRONMENT THAN IF THE OIL HAD BEEN LEFT ALONE. USE OF THESE AGENTS WITHOUT THE PERMISSION OF THE CAPTAIN OF THE PORT IS AGAINST THE LAW. YOU MAY BE PENALIZED UP TO $32,500 FOR EACH INCIDENT!!

Of course, if you think about what goes down your drains and toilets, onto your lawn, and into your city's gutters, you'll realize that a lot more than just surfactants is washing into the Gulf. Several million pounds of herbicides enter the Gulf annually, mostly from the Mississippi. "It's always been considered the waste disposal chute," the Tulane/Xavier Center for Bioenvironmental Research's John McLachlan told the *Times-Picayune*. "One of the things we know is that almost any pharmaceutical taken by human beings or given to livestock or chickens ends up in wastewater and eventually in the river." That includes estrogen from all those birth control pills, which occurs in the river in concentrations high enough to feminize fish. Don't worry about this depressing the fish; there's plenty of Prozac and other antidepressants in that water, too.

Then, of course, there is the dead zone, which stretches out from the mouth of the Mississippi to blanket most of the Louisiana coast. A "dead zone" is an area of the sea with so little oxygen that few animals can survive in it. A few such places occur naturally, usually in locations with stagnant water, but there are currently more than four hundred dead zones around the world, and humans are responsible for 99 percent of them, including the mother of all dead zones, the Gulf of Mexico's, which in 2010 covered nearly eight thousand square miles—an area larger than the state of New Jersey, nearly devoid of life.

Dead zones form when nutrient runoff from cities and agricultural fertilizers spark runaway algae blooms. As rivers sweep the nutrients to the coasts, all that nitrogen and phosphorus grows algae instead of corn and pigs. As I explained in chapter 3, a moderate amount of algae in estuaries is a good thing, but when massive algae blooms die, they are consumed by bacteria, which use oxygen to do this. Big-enough algae blooms spark population explosions of bacteria that suck every milliliter of oxygen out of the water. Any animal trapped in such a zone dies. Even chronically low oxygen levels, those not low enough to kill, can cause severe reproduction problems for fish.

The Gulf dead zone has been around for some time, but it is growing worse, thanks to warmer temperatures and Midwest farmers dumping increasing amounts of chemical fertilizer on their fields in the desperate attempt to keep them productive. The five largest dead zones of all time have occurred in the past decade. One of the reasons shrimping has become less profitable in the Gulf is because offshore shrimpers have to travel farther, crossing the dead zone to get to live fishing grounds.

Even close to shore, dead zones occur with alarming frequency. In early September 2010, Bayou Chaland, on the west side of the mouth of the Mississippi River, became a river of dead fish. No water was visible, just a silver ribbon of menhaden carcasses curling out of sight. Water temperatures were pushing high into the nineties, and the Mississippi was clogged with runoff and algae. There was no oxygen to be had.

To me, the sad case of menhaden sums up the irony of the dead zone. Menhaden are small, silvery herring cousins that do something few other adult fish do: They eat plankton directly, swimming with their mouths open and filtering it out of the water with their gills. They are the offshore counterpart to oysters, darting along the coasts like little Shop-Vacs, cleaning the water. And they occur in massive schools of millions of fish. One of my favorite sounds on my sailing trip was the nightly *plink, plink* of uncountable menhaden breaking the surface. Doing similar work all along the Atlantic and Gulf coasts for millennia, menhaden once kept plankton concentrations manageable, converting it into protein and fish oil. These small, bony, smelly oil capsules are prized food for bluefish, redfish, mackerel, tuna, striped bass, seagulls, pelicans—and you. If your omega-3 supplement was made with fish oil, that oil probably came from menhaden. They are also the darling of the fishmeal industry. Being so high in protein (which is part nitrogen) and omega-3 fats, and easy to catch by the ton, they are the perfect food for everything from salmon to poultry. And there's the irony. The menhaden that should be vacuuming the excess plankton from the Gulf and reducing the dead zone aren't there in sufficient abundance because they've been scooped up in nets and fed to chickens in the massive poultry and egg factories of the Midwest, where their nitrogen flows through the bodies of hens and into the Mississippi River watershed, where it washes into the Gulf and fuels the growth of algae blooms not eaten by the missing menhaden.

Dead zones are not new. Mobile Bay has a long tradition known as a jubilee. Almost every summer, and sometimes several times per year, a night will come when the winds die and the air is perfectly still. Suddenly, in the predawn hours, fish and crabs swarm the edge of the bay, sometimes flopping right onto the beach. Crabs crawl out of the water, making no attempt to get away. The tide line becomes one continuous, speckled footpath of flounder. Calls go out, bells are rung, and residents race to shore for the easy pickings. The naturalist Archie Carr described the abundance: "At a good jubilee you can quickly fill a washtub with shrimp. You can gig a hundred flounders and fill the back of your pickup truck a foot deep in crabs."

Jimbo Meador has experienced jubilees all his life. "When you see those little eels wriggling at the edge, you know something's about to happen," he told me. His home, on the eastern shore of Mobile Bay, is ground zero for jubilees, and he and a friend recently stumbled on one in progress.

What is happening is that Mobile Bay, home to cities, farms, factories, and countless septic systems, has its own little sporadic dead zone. Under normal conditions, enough water mixes in the shallow bay to keep even the low areas oxygenated. But when temperatures are warm and the wind dies, the mucky bottom runs out of oxygen. Then bottom-swelling species like flounder and crabs follow the oxygen, desperate to breathe. On really bad nights, this leaves them gasping at the edge of their world. Jubilee!

Reports of jubilees date back to the 1860s, but they seem to be growing more frequent and intense. "As a kid, I never saw anything die during a jubilee," Jimbo said. "Now we see things die."

That's a variation on a sentiment I heard from people throughout the Gulf region during my travels there. Things used to be a certain way. And now they're not like that anymore.

Chapter 10

PLACELESSNESS

ON A LATE-SUMMER morning, as the sun baked a strange wetness out of the asphalt of St. Charles Avenue and streetcars hissed past, I ducked into the air-conditioned cave of Serio's Po-Boys & Deli and ordered an oyster po' boy from the guy at the counter, who turned out to be Mike Serio, the owner. The guy in line behind me turned out to have played ball for Louisiana State University—no surprise, since Serio's is a temple to LSU sports—and we slipped into a good three-way conversation as we chugged iced tea and the line behind us grew. I was feeling good about my decision to beat the crowd to an early lunch when my po' boy arrived from the back—plump, golden, sizzling fried oysters stuffed into split French bread with a little mayo, lettuce, and tomato. Po' boys can be just about anything stuffed into French bread, even roast beef, but the sandwich's reputation rests on the oyster version, which is why I was here, Serio's having been a New Orleans po' boy institution for more than fifty years. In that time, oysters had become less abundant, and the sandwich's moniker now applied to your postprandial finances. Mine set me back fourteen bucks.

Right behind my po' boy came the cook, a heavyset older guy shouldering an impressive air of resignation. "That's it," he said to the counter staff, waving his hands in front of him. "No more oysters."

All eyes in line turned to me. "No more today?" I asked hopefully.

"No more never," he said, breathing heavily, then turned and shuffled back into the kitchen.

Mike Serio sighed and said not "never," just until he could find a new source for oysters. *If* he could find a new source. The football player shook his head. I clutched my po' boy, skulked off to a dark corner table, and chowed down, a runnel of mayo and hot oyster juice dripping out of the low end of the sandwich. At the counter, there was a run on shrimp po' boys.

What makes a place a place? What builds its character? And how does it hold on to that character when everything changes? Those were my thoughts as I stepped out of Serio's, turned left, and crossed Canal Street. With its heavy air and palm trees, Canal Street felt underwater to me, like a scene from *20,000 Leagues Under the Sea*, complete with giant sea anemones.

Across Canal Street was the French Quarter, the Vieux Carré. This was the area first settled, the high ground least likely to flood. Even so, it flooded during extreme high water, which is why the founders built their initial three-foot levee in the 1700s, pushing the waters onto their lower neighbors. Relations between the high-ground and low-ground dwellers have been complicated ever since.

I wandered Royal Street past the branch of the New Orleans Police Department and cut down Toulouse Street to Decatur Street and Jackson Square, ground zero for the French Quarter.

Jackson Square's elegant gardens are bounded on the north by the classy restraint of St. Louis Cathedral and on the south by the French Market, which began life in 1791 as an American Indian trading post and later became a real farmer's market selling the dazzling array of goods that came into the city. Now it's an open-air mall and food court catering to tourists who throng Café du Monde for overpriced café au lait. Fortune-tellers, horse-drawn carriages, and silver-skinned mimes work the crowd that spills onto the street.

I'm not sure what I think about the French Quarter. The wrought-iron balconies? Gorgeous. The music? Genuine. The air of lassitude and decay? Alluring. But I get uneasy in places whose primary concern is my entertainment. If the measure of a town's integrity is the percentage of its shops that cater to locals, then the French Quarter does not score well. It's about seventy-five blocks of beignets, souvenirs, and pralines—a candy so cloying that it must be for tourists, because I can't imagine that anybody who's had one goes back for a second. At night, quite a few of those blocks devote themselves to beer and strippers. I once found myself in the city at the same time as a national Lutheran youth convention. Thousands of fresh-faced teens mobbed the city in identical lime-green T-shirts. Watching groups of them walk Bourbon Street, sidestepping drunks and staring in perplexity at the neon sign for Big Daddy's World Famous Love Acts, gave me complex feelings about America.

There's nothing wrong with socking it to the tourists. They have turned up, almost desperate to part with their money, so why not help them out? Thirty-eight billion dollars flow into the Gulf Coast annually from people wanting to escape their regular lives for a few days. More than five hundred thousand residents— five times as many as work in the oil industry—work in Gulf

Coast tourism. The reason all those tourists endure airport security lines and rental car chicanery is to go somewhere *different*. To experience a different climate, culture, landscape, mind-set. To get a sense, even just for a little while, of what life is like in this other place. Otherwise, why leave home?

More so than any other American city, New Orleans has always traded on its mystique. People flocked to the city to get a taste of that distinctive style. Life was different there, thanks to factors that had been set in motion hundreds of years ago. There was the collision of cultures—French, Acadian, American Indian, Spanish, African. And there was a collision of lifestyles, which is what you get when you set a major port town in a relatively lawless area. Jean Lafitte and other pirates and privateers smuggled stolen goods into the city by poling their pirogues up Bayou Lafourche, slipping into the city by the back door and bypassing the customs agents manning the mouth of the river. Legal goods came downriver from farms and upriver from shrimpers and oystermen working the salt marshes. Rum and slaves arrived from the Caribbean. Most of all, there was the ambience of the place. The air was different. The land was different—or, rather, almost nonexistent. It was America's swamp city.

New Orleans is still a swamp city, as becomes alarmingly apparent when you fly into Louis Armstrong New Orleans International Airport. You see the Gulf of Mexico. You see Lake Pontchartrain. You see the Mississippi. In between these landmarks, you see trees, but the sun reflects back at you through the trees, following your plane, because the ground is all water, too. The city pokes out of the mush like a clump of oversize cypress.

All of this is lost on the tourists mobbing Jackson Square, who have no idea that they've come to New Orleans because it is America's premier wetlands city. There have been too many levels of remove, too much packaging. They don't understand that the reason they eat raw oysters and shrimp jambalaya, the reason they listen to jazz at Preservation Hall and follow the Zulu parade, the reason they puke rum drinks into their hotel room commodes at two A.M., the reason Hurricane Katrina became America's greatest engineering nightmare, all has to do with the city's geography.

Maybe they don't want to know. For a real understanding of the forces that have shaped, and continue to shape, the city, they could go take a look at where the Seventeenth Street Canal levee gave way (one of fifty-three breaches) after Katrina, or they could skip the flea market stands of the French Market and go to the Crescent City Farmer's Market, one of the only farmer's markets I know where you can load up on shrimp, softshell crabs, black drum, and other seafood. Other options, even closer at hand, will also give a glimpse into the working guts of the city.

One is a handsome set of steps rising right beside the French Market. It leads to the Moonwalk, a plaza named for former mayor Maurice "Moon" Landrieu. The Moonwalk's primary attraction is that it allows you to see something you otherwise can't in New Orleans—the Mississippi River. Staring down at Ol' Muddy from the Moonwalk, watching the giant container ships navigate its curves, one of the first things you notice is that the river is about as high as the cars parked in lots beneath the Moonwalk. This explains why, unlike in other cities built on great rivers, where you stroll along a sidewalk and look *down* on the river, in New Orleans you have to climb up onto the levees to see the river, because it is higher than the city. If this strikes you as an ill-advised design, well, you aren't the first person to think so.

Half of greater New Orleans is below sea level, which puts it well below the height of the Mississippi, which ranges from a few feet above sea level to a flood crest as high as eighteen feet above. The French Quarter is actually in pretty good position, because its natural levees are about fourteen feet above sea level—the same height as the typical flood crest on the river. Two blocks away from the levees, St. Louis Cathedral is eight feet above sea level. From there, the land drops off fast. Even the field of the Superdome is just three feet above sea level, considerably lower than the average height of the river. As John McPhee memorably described it in the *New Yorker* twenty-four years ago, "if somehow the ships could turn and move at river level into the city and into the stadium they would hover above the playing field like blimps." Poorer areas of the city were developed in even lower, swampier lands. The notorious Ninth Ward is, on average, seven feet below sea level. The entire area between the Mississippi River and Lake Pontchartrain resembles a giant bowl floating on the water, its lip protruding above the surface and keeping the rest dry. The levees that have been built along the river and the lake are simply a way of raising that lip, buying some time. But it is only a limited amount of time, because every year, the bowl sinks a little more while the waters around it rise.

Somewhere north of Baton Rouge, the bedrock of North America tilts downward and dips toward the Gulf of Mexico. Like a gigantic and gradual boat ramp, it slopes into the Gulf, forming the continental shelf—an underwater sill that extends about forty miles out. For its entire existence, the Mississippi River has been unloading onto this ramp—first, when the seas were higher, at the top of the ramp, now about halfway down—and covering it with mud. A lot of mud. New Orleans sits on soft sediment nearly five miles deep. The current mouth of the

Mississippi, ninety-five miles farther downstream, sits on eight miles of the stuff. This slope of goo is literally sliding into the Gulf of Mexico at a rate of two millimeters per year. Occasionally, when the goo skids and quivers, this causes an earthquake.

As you might imagine, the lack of bedrock presents architectural challenges. Where most of the rest of the country makes its buildings secure by anchoring them to bedrock, in southern Louisiana there is no rock to anchor to. Instead, engineers resort to what is known as "friction pilings"—columns driven so deep into the mud that the force of friction holds them in place. In this way, the Superdome and other buildings in New Orleans float atop a sea of goo, about as permanent as riverboat casinos.

It isn't entirely accurate to call the stuff beneath New Orleans mud, because virtually all the water was long ago squeezed out of it, but it isn't entirely inaccurate either. There's still a little water and space that can be squeezed out, a little more compaction that can happen. Thus New Orleans keeps sinking. Many spots in the city sink an inch per year. Pumps must force water out of the city at all times. Many of its levees have sunk more than three feet in forty years—a factor in their failure during Hurricane Katrina, since, of course, the Mississippi River has not sunk at all.

Standing atop the Moonwalk, seeing the river surge past, you realize that the far-flung bayou communities aren't the only ones in the wetland-restoration fight. From space, the delta looks like a bunch of tattered clothes hanging in the Gulf, and a lot of these tatters simply disintegrate in the rinse cycle of each hurricane. In the summer of 2005, Katrina and Rita hacked off 217 square miles of wetland in just a few days. The U.S. Geological Survey's rule of thumb is that every 2.5 miles of wetland reduces a foot of storm surge. Southern Louisiana's remaining wetlands reduced Katrina's monstrous twenty-eight-foot storm surge by six feet—

giving a horrible hint of what future storms could do—but its original wetlands might have cut that storm surge by much more. At least, they might have if the notorious MR. GO canal hadn't given the storm the keys to the city.

In 2009, MR. GO was closed to protect New Orleans, but future storms will have direct access to the city from almost any direction. At some point later in this century, New Orleans will disappear beneath the waves, an American Atlantis. Much of Louisiana south of I-10 will be sliced clean off the United States, and you'll have gorgeous coastal views as you drive along Pontchartrain Bay.

If the river isn't enough of a cold splash of reality, tourists can wander six blocks north of Jackson Square to 1039 Toulouse Street, the home of P&J Oysters. P&J Oysters has held down this block, on the northern edge of the French Quarter, since 1921. To me, it is essential to the Quarter's integrity, because it is the last industrially zoned building there. For ninety years, men have been shucking oysters in the numbered stalls of P&J, delivering them by the gallon to restaurants throughout New Orleans and, formerly, throughout the country. The shucking floor is open to the street, and it has always been a de facto attraction. "We get tourists here all the time," Al Sunseri, president of P&J, told me when I stopped in. "They stick their heads in. The little carriages all stop here. I don't know what they told them about us, because they've never come in and asked, but they loved it because you'd get that fresh, clean sea smell right here downtown. The floor was always wet. Now it's not wet. Feels kinda weird."

The floor was not wet because P&J was shut down. A few workers were repainting the walls. Otherwise it was quiet. After

134 years in the oyster business, 90 in this historic spot, after weathering wars and hurricanes and seismic shifts in the market, P&J was laid low by the oil spill. There were no oysters to be had.

"We're working with the city to make sure we maintain our zoning," Al said. "If we don't operate, we could lose it. Which would be wrong for a number of reasons. This is really the last urban oyster house you're gonna find. Not just in New Orleans, but in the country. You're not gonna find another right in its old, historic downtown. They had 'em! Baltimore had 'em! Hartford had 'em! But they don't anymore. We're really the last. And it's of no fault of ours that we're not working right now. We were rolling right along."

Learn the history of P&J and you'll grasp a lot of the history of both New Orleans and the oyster business. The company was founded by John Popich, a young Croatian immigrant, in 1876. Popich cultivated and distributed his oysters to area restaurants for a quarter of a century before taking on a partner, another Croat named Joseph Jurisich, so that Popich could farm the oysters while Jurisich handled distribution. Popich & Jurisich Oyster Dealers found their Toulouse Street shucking house in 1921 and took on a young salesman named Alfred Sunseri. Sunseri was in the banana business, distributing bananas throughout the country for the United Fruit Company, the forerunner of Chiquita. The bananas arrived in New Orleans by boat from South America and the Caribbean and were shipped by Railway Express—the Federal Express of its day, with a countrywide network of refrigerated train cars. "That's how we got involved in this," Al (grandson of the original Al) told me. "My family was in the banana business. We had all these customers built in. We just started selling oysters to the same hotels, restaurants, and grocery stores that we were selling bananas to. And they were shipped the exact same way—on the train."

Three times a day, barrels of live oysters from the oyster grounds arrived in the city—at Basin Street Wharf if they were coming from the east side of the river, and at Governor Nicholls Street Wharf if they were coming from the west side of the river—and were rolled straight onto train cars. Jars of shucked oysters came from P&J's shucking house. This was the era when Chesapeake oysters were declining, because of overharvesting, and Gulf oysters were ascendant. And P&J became one of the largest oyster dealers in the South. "We had contracts with the Army and Navy. We sold to A&P. It was big!"

That all came to an end in 1961, when Railway Express failed, outcompeted by refrigerated trucks. Large wholesale brokers began buying directly from the oystermen when the boats came in, loading trailer trucks, and shipping them out, bypassing the city of New Orleans entirely. P&J Oysters was left with only its New Orleans accounts.

Still, this is a city that can eat a lot of oysters. "We started small," Al explained, "built ourselves up to being one of the biggest in the South, and then Railway Express ended and we dropped back down to the middle, but now we've been on an incline for years. We're not national like we were; we're very localized. But we handle a significant number of oysters. Our little company shucks thirty-five thousand oysters a day, and sells another twenty thousand to thirty-five thousand in the shell."

Or, rather, it did. Within weeks of the spill, most of the oyster grounds on both sides of the Mississippi River—the richest oyster grounds in the world—were closed for fear of contamination. Unable to get oysters, P&J closed down its operation and laid off most of its shuckers. Restaurants in the city stopped serving oyster po' boys. The repercussions of the oyster shut-down vibrated across the country, well beyond the restaurant industry, from the guy who used to sell hundreds of thousands of reused coffee bags every month to oyster harvesters to bag their catch, to the guy who used to buy the calcium-rich shell for chicken feed throughout the Midwest, to the road projects waiting on oyster shell for their subsurface.

And what happened next is one of the deepest ironies in a tale rife with them. An astonishing number of the Mississippi River Delta's oysters died. Some reefs suffered mortalities of 90 percent. It was one of the most heartbreaking and massive wipeouts of a population you'll ever hear about. But it was not the oil that killed them.

The story starts with the leveeing of the Mississippi. Once the bayous and other distributaries of the great river were sealed off, and all that freshwater stopped trickling through the marshes, their salinity changed. The salt moved north. Freshwater marshes became salt marshes. Salt marshes became open water.

For oystermen, that whole stretch of the 1800s and 1900s was a challenge. Oysters thrive in brackish water. In freshwater their membranes stop functioning and they die. Fully saline, oceanic water holds predators that love to eat thin-shelled baby oysters. Those predators can't survive in brackish water, which is why oysters thrive in that mid-salinity zone amid the marshes, tucked away at the underwater fringes of the grasses.

As the salinity of the Mississippi River Delta changed, rich oyster grounds became death zones for the bivalves. But new oyster reefs appeared in formerly freshwater marshes that had become suitably brackish. Some oystermen wound up holding leases on useless grounds. Others adjusted and moved north, fol-lowing the salinity.

Meanwhile, deprived of sediment, all the marshlands were sinking, reducing the amount of oyster grounds. Only about half of Louisiana's original oyster reefs remain, though that still is tops in the world.

But it is not what it used to be, in more ways than one. As we sat in his office, watching two guys paint a room that should have been filled with shell and shuckers and wet with oyster juice, Al Sunseri made damn sure I understood that. "The oysters don't get fat like they used to," he said. "Because of the deterioration of the marsh due to oil and gas exploration and the levees. There's nothing to block the saltwater anymore. You get these salinity changes all over the place. Now, when the saltwater comes in from the south, it purges them. Years ago, I was going deep-sea fishing for red snapper with a friend of mine. We picked two sacks of beautiful, fat oysters from the oyster grounds behind Lake Washington, in Port Sulfur, and took 'em with us. When we got out to the rig, we hung the oysters overboard in baskets. We didn't have them in the water an hour, and when we pulled 'em back in, they were skinny and bitter salty. They'd shot out every bit of juice that was in 'em. And I'm telling you, these were some fat oysters. Skinny. And *bitter* salty."

Al also cleared up a mystery for me. In the rest of North America, and in all of Europe, oysters are always named for the bay they come from. Apalachicola, Wellfleet, Malpeque, Chesapeake. The tradition evolved because people recognized that the place made the oyster. As filter feeders, oysters spend all day with their shells cracked open, pumping as much as fifty gallons of water a day through their gills and filtering out the phytoplankton, along with other tiny particles, for their food. In doing so, they take on and concentrate the flavors of their bay. A Wellfleet tastes like the briny North Atlantic. A Chesapeake has the sweet funk of Appalachian rivers. Yet all oysters from Texas to Alabama are sold simply as Gulf oysters, as if the ninth-largest body of water on Earth had no diversity worth mentioning, no bays with individual character. I asked Al why.

"Let me tell you something," he said. "We *did* name oysters for where they come from. We did, too. And that all changed." There were always oyster grounds on both sides of the Mississippi River below New Orleans, Al explained. The marshes on the east side were fresher, and those on the west side were saltier. The east side made good predator-free nursery grounds for baby oysters, and the west side was good for "salting up" the oysters. "You'd take oysters from the public grounds on the east side of the river and transport them through Empire Locks to your leases on the west side. That's how you did it."

And in those west-side bays, the oysters got incredibly delicious. "If you could see what it used to be like," Al said, shaking his head. He wasn't nostalgic; he's too hard-nosed a businessman for that. He just had the well-weathered disgust of having had a front-row seat to watch the state kill its golden goose. "Something about the Plaquemines–Jefferson Parish area is so rich. You had all that marsh going out there. Beautiful oysters—the sweetest, saltiest oysters. We called 'em candy oysters. They had all these different flavors. Some had a woody flavor. Some had a grassy taste. They all had that firm, thick eye, sometimes as big as half of the oyster, because they were so healthy." The eye is the muscle the oyster uses to close its shell. It's the same muscle we eat in a scallop, and it's responsible for a lot of an oyster's sweetness and texture. A "big-eyed" oyster is like a molluscan weightlifter. "A number of different areas on the west side of the river produced that kind of oyster: Grand Bayou, Bayou Cook, Lake Washington, Lake Grand Ecaille. Our company made its name off of them. Our card had those bays on it. People asked for those oysters by name. Every so often, when conditions were right, you'd get nice oysters on the east side of the river, with these beautiful golden shells and nice big eyes, but only certain times of the year. It wasn't like on the west side."

With their long-standing relationships with different growers, P&J would carefully buy from different areas at different times of year, harvesting the oysters when they were at their peak. "In years gone by, you knew which areas you'd be buying from certain times of the year, and you'd plan that way. So you'd have oysters from Caminada Bay and Bayou Cook at a certain time, and then at another time you might have some Lake Washington and Basin Bois and Bay Batiste oysters. That's how it was. You'd move around."

Then Railway Express went under and the big brokers and trucking companies moved in. And they weren't interested in where the oysters were from. "These food service people didn't care what was in the container. They just put a number on it. When you have a trailer truck of oysters, that's four hundred sacks. You might have oysters from four, five, six different fishermen. And they're all being sold as one lot. That broker's not selling Bayou Cook oysters, because he's selling ten, fifteen truckloads of oysters a day, piling the good ones with the bad. He's selling widgets. So instead of people thinking about Bayou Cook, Grand Bayou, Grand Lake oysters, they started saying Louisiana oysters. *Gulf* oysters."

Thus began the practice of selling almost tasteless oysters harvested directly from the public grounds on the east side. "No one sold directly from the public grounds. We always moved them to places like Bayou Cook and Grand Bayou to fatten up. And it changed."

Even more disturbing, the places themselves changed. In the past fifty years, those beautiful oyster grounds on the west side of the river have changed drastically, just like the places I saw on my boat ride through Terrebonne Parish with Kadoo. Today, Grand Lake and Lake Grand Ecaille are not lakes; they are the edge of the Gulf of Mexico.

Al minces no words about what did it. "Navigational canals. The MR. GO brings saltwater all the way into New Orleans. It just funnels right on in. And you got the Barataria Waterway. If you make it a straight route, it makes shipping a lot easier. I used to work offshore out of Vermilion Bay, and it was hard getting out there, going through all those channels and locks and things. A lot of that shipping's oil and gas related. You've got these deep-channel waterways, and they just funnel the saltwater. They start off narrow and end up wide, and the impact becomes enormous. Then you've got ten thousand miles of pipeline canals. Look at aerial photos from 1940, and then look again today."

We did. The two maps were unrecognizable. It looked like someone had imported the original image into Photoshop and gone crazy with the Eraser feature. The familiar Louisiana shape of U.S. maps and road atlases is a fantasy; it depicts a state that hasn't existed since the 1930s.

Al didn't begrudge the oil companies their business. "I'm no environmentalist by any means. I'm a huge supporter of oil and gas. We all use it. We need it. I mean, look around this office. Look at all the things made from petroleum products. We need it. But you know what? There's enough money being made that they should be able to do the right thing. If the state had been good stewards of our money, and had followed the law, then we wouldn't be looking at ten-thousand-plus miles of pipeline. And we wouldn't be looking at abandoned wells. It just goes back to the power of the oil and gas industries. They have extreme power."

In this case, the power to ignore the law. "There's laws on the books! They're supposed to fill in the canals. For nearly twenty years, they haven't followed the law. You know why? Because the permitting department that gives permits to the oil and gas companies is the same department that oversees coastal restoration—the Department of Natural Resources. *Waaaay* too cozy. It's just like what happened with the Minerals Management Service. That's in federal waters, but the same thing goes on in state waters. It goes back to Huey Long! Every single one of those pipeline canals should have been filled in, but they don't like to, in case they have to repair them, and the [DNR] secretary has the authority to not require them to. They're supposed to maintain the integrity of the state! What the hell? How can they let those things go?"

Throughout the twentieth century, oystermen responded to the loss of their traditional grounds much as the oysters themselves did—by following the salt and creeping northward, ever closer to the levees themselves. Both bivalves and growers established themselves in brackish areas that would have been too fresh for oysters before the levee system was built. And they continued to call for freshwater diversions to restore brackish conditions to the areas that had become too salty.

In 1991 they got their wish, when the Caernarvon Freshwater Diversion became the first construction on the river to purposely divert water out of the main channel for the benefit of oysters. It worked for the oysters, and it built land as a bonus. (Although, as New Orleans environmental lawyer Oliver Houck pointed out, after Katrina, "the newly restored marshes of the $80 million Caernarvon diversion project ended up on rooftops in St. Bernard.")

Caernarvon was so popular that seven other diversions projects followed, this time expressly for coastal restoration. Oystermen screamed, as some of their new best grounds were threatened with freshness, and diversion plans were sometimes held up until their needs were accommodated. One notorious project, the Davis Pond Freshwater Diversion, was created in 1992 to send water to the west side of the river into Barataria Basin and some of P&J's best oyster grounds. Because of design flaws, it was more or less inoperable from its construction until 2007, when things were finally straightened out. Davis Pond had never been operated fullbore until it was called to emergency service after the oil spill.

And this is where yet another irony kicks in. On April 25, as ranks of black goo from the Macondo well crept toward the marshes of the Mississippi River Delta, Governor Bobby Jindal ordered the state to open the diversion gates on the river full blast, hoping that the force of all that water surging through the marshes would push the oil back out to sea. Caernarvon was opened all the way, as was Davis Pond. On May 7, Office of Coastal Protection and Restoration assistant director Jerome Zeringue (the same official who had explained why Isle de Jean Charles couldn't be saved by the Morganza to the Gulf levee project), announced, "We have opened every diversion structure we control on the state and parish level." Caernarvon, with a flow of 8,800 cubic feet per second of water, and Davis Pond, with 10,650 cubic feet per second, were the two monsters, but the seven diversions combined sent an impressive 30,000 cubic feet per second of muddy water (about 5 percent of the river) churning into the delta marshes.

There was about as much science behind Jindal's decision as there was behind his later plan to build new sand islands in the Gulf to wall off the oil. In other words, none. Maybe the diversions helped keep the oil offshore, and maybe they didn't. Barataria Basin and Breton Sound, the main targets of this freshwater salvation, were some of the places most heavily oiled. Perhaps they would have been even more oiled without the diversions, or perhaps, as one oysterman suggested, the outflow had created a huge circular current that sucked oil into the marshes on the backswing. No one will ever know for sure.

What we do know is that the freshwater killed more oysters than any event in the history of Louisiana. Over the past century, most of the state's best oyster grounds had crept up into once-fresh areas now brackish, and dangerously close to the levees. And now the freshwater came back with a vengeance.

In July, after the diversions had been blasting for about seventy-five days, Patrick Banks, oyster manager for the Louisiana Department of Wildlife and Fisheries, surveyed public oyster grounds on the east side of the river. The reefs were "fallow," in his terms—dead, at least temporarily. Earl Melancon, an oyster specialist at Lafourche Parish's Nicholls State University, explained, "If you lose an oyster reef, it takes three years minimum to get it back into production." That's how long it takes new oyster larvae that settle onto the dead shells to reach market size.

Banks next checked reefs on the west side of the river, where P&J gets 95 percent of its oysters, and found mortality rates of around 60 percent. Melancon, who has been working with

Louisiana's oysters for thirty years, surveyed Barataria Basin on July 20 and found even worse destruction. Up to 90 percent of the oysters were dead in the upper parts of the bay. "One of the worst mortalities I've seen," Melancon said. The gaping shells were pearly white inside, with no barnacle growth, indicating fresh deaths. Salinity levels in the upper bay averaged about 3 parts per thousand—virtually fresh, and lethal for oysters. Ninety-degree water temperatures didn't help.

In southern parts of Barataria Basin, farther from the Davis Pond Diversion, salinity levels measured 5 to 14 parts per thousand, and the oysters were hanging on, with moderate mortality rates. Perhaps these oysters, so close to the Gulf, had been saved from the oil, but only at the expense of the much greater reefs to the north.

Further complicating the picture, in September, Mississippi's Department of Marine Resources sampled oyster reefs in the state—where, of course, there were no freshwater diversions—and found 80 to 90 percent mortality in some places, the worst ever recorded in Mississippi. Oil had been seen on those reefs earlier in the summer, but it was unclear whether the oil or the scorching summer was more to blame.

Little oil was found in the vicinity of the Barataria Basin oyster reefs, but that doesn't mean oysters in the area weren't picking up any of it. Because they are filter feeders, and because dispersed oil is about the same size as the plankton they eat, oysters are quite good at absorbing it. Wilma Subra, a chemist working for the Louisiana Environmental Action Network, sampled oysters near the mouth of the Mississippi River on August 3 and found that they contained a stomach-churning 12,500 milligrams of hydrocarbons per kilogram of total weight. That means 1.25 percent of their bodies was composed of oil. The sediment in the estuaries was also full of contaminants.

By September many Louisiana oyster areas had been re-opened to harvesting. But there was little to harvest. What was available followed the ineluctable rules of supply and demand: Sacks of oysters soared in price from twenty-four dollars per sack in 2009 to fifty-eight dollars per sack in 2010. Overall, up to half of Louisiana's oysters may have been killed by the open-ing of the diversions. Since the state has two million acres of oyster reefs, and a single acre of reef can easily hold a million oysters, it's possible that a *trillion* oysters perished in this artifi-cial Great Flood. It will take years for the reefs to recover to a point where they can again be harvested.

And that leaves P&J Oysters with virtually no product. In August, Al Sunseri was down to two drivers and two workers, bringing in oysters from out of state to keep a handful of old clients in shellfish. The same was true throughout the city of New Orleans, leaving the home of oysters Rockefeller and oys-ters Bienville and, yes, oyster po' boys in danger of becoming something . . . less. Casamento's, New Orleans' most iconic oys-ter bar, home of what *Playboy* magazine calls "the best fried oysters in the world," was considering importing oysters from Apalachicola, Florida, to replace its usual P&J supply—if even those were available. "We've never ever gone one or two days without oysters," owner C. J. Gerdes said. "We've closed early, we've had some problems when the beds shut down or the red tide came, and we opened late after Katrina, but we've never not had oysters." Felix's Oyster Bar was using Texas and Florida oysters. Many other restaurants, including the entire Red Lob-ster chain, had simply scratched oysters altogether as they watched supplies dwindle and prices skyrocket. Susan Spicer, a well-known New Orleans chef, brought a lawsuit against BP, saying, "Oysters are part of everyone's upbringing. It's family history. It's unthinkable, a future without them."

Of course, New Orleans is more than just oysters. Its complex and delightful mix of cultures, cuisines, and neighborhoods will continue beyond the oil spill. But if a number of establishments turn to Cisco trucks for their seafood supply, if P&J can't claw back into the business and 1039 Toulouse Street becomes another praline store, then some of the color will have faded from this most colorful of cities.

Chapter 11

BP IS MY COPILOT

NOT LONG AFTER the *Deepwater Horizon* exploded, the Obama administration imposed a six-month moratorium on deepwater oil production in the Gulf of Mexico, intending to study the situation and come up with some revised safety guidelines. In response, the Louisiana Oil and Gas Association quietly put together an event called the Rally for Economic Survival at the Cajundome in Lafayette, Louisiana. Eleven thousand people packed the place to hear the governor, lieutenant governor, and, of all people, the executive director of the Louisiana Seafood Promotion and Marketing Board rail against Obama for stealing their jobs. Nobody blamed BP or Transocean. Nobody wanted more safety regulations. Fire up the rigs, they cried. Drill, baby, drill. I listened in disbelief as the anger rose to a fever pitch and eleven thousand Gulf Coasters screamed for their own annihilation.

"Enough is enough!" raged Lieutenant Governor Scott Angelle in his thick Cajun accent. "It is time to stop punishing innocent American workers to achieve some unrealistic political agenda. Louisiana has a long and strong, distinguished history of fueling America, and we proudly do what few other states are willing to do. Each and every day . . . we put on our hard hats and our steel-toed boots, we kiss our families good-bye, and we begin the tough work of exploring, producing, processing, storing, refining, and transporting the fuel to energize the great United States of America. While we too support the use of renewable and alternative energy, let's keep the conversation real. America is not yet ready to get all its fuel from the birds and the bees and the flowers and the trees!"

True. But claiming that Louisiana fuels America is kind of like claiming that the gas station attendant supplies your gas. Of the six to seven billion barrels of oil consumed by the United States each year, about 10 percent comes from Federal Gulf of Mexico waters—the same amount that comes from the Persian Gulf. Louisiana itself is no longer a significant source of crude, onshore or offshore. It supplies only about 1 percent—on a par with Oklahoma or North Dakota. What it does supply is cheap labor and a pliant government. "Today, we tell Congress that we 'sacrificed' ourselves for the national good," Oliver Houck wrote in the *Tulane Environmental Law Journal*. "Never has there been such a willing, complicit sacrifice. We made a bundle of money, wasted most of it, and blackballed anyone who questioned what it was doing to the Louisiana coast. About 70 years ago, Louisiana made a deal with the oil and gas industry. The industry would get what it wanted; the state would get a piece of the take."

Today, it barely gets that. Of the more than $5 billion received by the federal government in offshore royalties in 2009, only $222,725 went to Louisiana. Terrebonne Parish, for all its tough work exploring, producing, processing, storing, refining, and transporting the fuel to energize the great United States of America, received a whopping $3,744 in compensation.

It's an old story, eerily reminiscent of tales in other places ruined by oil. You'd think that oil would bring prosperity to the places where it's discovered, and this myth is used to convince locals to turn over their lands to Big Oil, but in reality oil brings misery so dependably that economists even have a name for the phenomenon: the Resource Curse. Virtually everywhere oil is found, environmental and social degradation follow.

Ecuador, Venezuela, Iraq: Bad things happen to countries "blessed" with oil. The Niger Delta is the Mississippi River Delta's separated-at-birth twin, offering the best cautionary tale of all. This tropical river delta once held some of the greatest wetlands on Earth, with abundant shellfish, crabs, and shrimp that were the foundation of the economy and culture. It also harbored vast oil reserves beneath those wetlands, buried under millions of years' worth of river sediment. In the past fifty years, Shell has grown rich on that oil, while Nigeria—one of the ten oil-richest nations in the world—has become apocalyptic. Three times as much oil has spilled into the Niger Delta as was spilled by the *Deepwater Horizon*. The creeks are black and the crabs and shrimp are dead. Leaking, corroded wellheads dot the marshes. Gangs of rebels and oil thieves roam the jungle. Gas flares fill the air with mercury and arsenic. Disease is rampant. The government is a joke. In October 2010, the celebrations marking fifty years of Nigerian independence were wrecked by two car bombings by the Movement for the Emancipation of the Niger Delta (MEND) that killed twelve people. MEND had warned the government of the bombs days in advance—causing British dignitaries to stay away—but the government had ignored the warnings.

Southern Louisiana is no Nigeria, but it no longer quite resembles the United States, either. The trailer homes on pilings, the dearth of education, the chronic disease, the fat parish chiefs in thrall to their corporate masters; I know a banana republic when I see one.

So does Oliver Houck, who, in the *Nation*, described how Louisiana's "state brochures feature pelicans and oil platforms against the setting sun. The largest exhibit in New Orleans' Audubon Aquarium of the Americas contains the base of an oil rig, around which swim contented fish, framed by the logos of Shell, Chevron and BP." Cajuns have not grown rich on Gulf crude; Wall Street has. And all those petrodollars come at the expense of seafood dollars.

I'm sure Scott Angelle would argue that the oil industry is worth billions of dollars more than the seafood industry. But that's only because we haven't been sophisticated enough to put a value on the health savings from all that Gulf seafood, the hurricane protection from all those marshes. We can get oil from a hundred different places. What we can't get elsewhere are the Gulf's oyster reefs. *Best on the planet*. The wetlands. *Best on the planet*. How much are those sixteen thousand acres per year of disappearing land worth? What price the mental anxiety of a culture watching its homeland disintegrate? How much added value do you assign oyster reefs because they have never, ever blown up and killed the men working on them? It's only our inability to tally all the gains and losses that makes oil look good.

This is not simply a rhetorical argument. The science of both ecology and economics has advanced to the point that, for the first time, we can begin to assess "natural capital," to put numbers to some of these questions, and to show just how financially shortsighted the sacrifice of the Gulf has been.

Shortly before the oil spill, the nonprofit Earth Economics

produced *Gaining Ground*, the most comprehensive study of the economic value of an ecosystem ever undertaken. The ecosystem it chose to study just happened to be the Mississippi River Delta. The study asked one overarching, hard-nosed question: Would the costs of restoring the delta pay off? Would it be a good investment? Some of the economic benefits of delta restoration it considered included improved hurricane protection ("The less nature does its work, the more FEMA will be needed"), expanded fisheries, superior water quality, increased economic activity from tourism and recreation, and stability for "energy infrastructure." It took into account everything from the two hundred billion dollars in damages from Hurricane Katrina, to the costs to build water filtration plants when clean drinking water isn't available, to the price of shrimp. (Though it didn't even attempt to place a value on the potential loss of life in hurricanes, among other indirect effects.)

The conclusion? "Is this national investment worthwhile during a period of financial crisis? The results of this report point to an unequivocal 'yes.'" Wetlands are worth up to twelve thousand dollars per acre in annual benefits. The entire delta provides twelve billion to forty-seven billion dollars in *annual* benefits, depending on how you value various services. Over a century, that makes the delta worth more than a trillion dollars. (That's about ten times BP's market capitalization before the spill.) This trillion-dollar asset will be lost if we continue to practice business as usual.

Perhaps the question to ask is: Do we need to? In the days after the *Deepwater Horizon* explosion, as crude poured out of the hole in the Gulf floor, Bill Finch placed a provocative post on the Nature Conservancy's Web site:

Most of us console ourselves by blaming the companies, blaming the regulators, blaming the slow response, even as we continue to participate in that great conspiracy—every time we fill up our cars with Gulf Coast gas.

If you want to do something right now, do it with these numbers in mind:

- **59 gallons**: Average volume of motor vehicle gasoline used, per person per year, in Europe.
- **428 gallons**: Motor vehicle gasoline used, per person per year, in the United States.
- **620%**: Percentage by which U.S. gasoline usage for vehicles exceeds that of Europe.
- **9.989 million barrels**: Amount of oil used for gasoline each day in the United States.
- **1.8 million barrels of oil**: Amount of oil saved each day if U.S. gasoline consumption were only 500% greater than consumption in Europe.
- **1.75 million barrels of oil**: Amount of oil produced each day by all offshore wells in the Gulf of Mexico.

That's right. Simply reducing our gasoline consumption by 18 percent would eliminate our need for every drop of oil coming from the Gulf of Mexico. No wonder the Louisiana Oil and Gas Association is so freaked out. Gulf oil is a lot less essential than we are led to believe. If we each cut five or six miles of driving out of our daily schedule, we're there.

Still, we've been around this argument before, and as a group we've done virtually nothing to cut our addiction. Raise your hand if, after the *Exxon Valdez* spill in 1989, you made radical

BP IS MY COPILOT

changes in your lifestyle so that you wouldn't be part of the oil economy anymore. Neither did I. I shook my head, cursed Exxon, then hopped in my car and drove back to college. I was born into the oil economy and am no more capable of escaping it than a crab is capable of changing its ecosystem. None of us are. Is there an uglier oil spill than the slow-motion one spreading across the world in the form of blacktop? Condo parking lots, malls and discount stores, new roads. Even when we use our bicycles, we are using oil-dependent machines. The metal frame and components were mined with oil power, manufactured with oil power, delivered to stores with oil power. The tires, seats, and paint are made of petroleum. So are the roads they travel on. More oil goes into the production and transport of bikes in the United States than is saved by people using them to commute. They are a hell of a lot better than cars, but they are not an alternative system.

And realistically, most of us can't lead a normal life—earn a living, own a home, raise a family—without a car. It's built into the system. Give me a post-carbon community that's up and running, and I'll wave good-bye to all this and sign up tomorrow. But that community doesn't exist in the modern world. We can't opt out of antihistamines, glasses, toothbrushes, ink, roofing, electricity, or any of the other products made with petroleum. I use as little as possible. I buy as little as possible. I heat my house with wood—cut by a gas-powered chain saw and delivered by a gas-powered truck. There's no escape. Every time I warm my hands by the fire, drink a cup of coffee, or rest my head on a pillow, BP is right there beside me.

There's no escape for the oil companies either. They are as trapped by the system as we are. After the spill, the media seized on BP policies that rewarded managers for how much money they'd saved the company. So did Congress. In the hearings on the disaster, the congressional panel tried to force David Sims, a BP executive in charge of costs, to admit that cost was a consideration in safety decisions—which he eventually did. "Every conversation, every decision has a cost factor," Sims replied. "Every company that tries to be a company does that."

I agree. And BP is a publicly held company. Its job is to make money and funnel those profits to its shareholders. It has no moral responsibility to sacrifice profits in the name of environmental protection, safety, and the public good. It doesn't even have the option. Guess what happens to oil companies that are less profitable than their rivals? They disappear. Their stock prices plunge, and they soon get eaten by a rival. This is what happened to Amoco, Texaco, Gulf, and many others. The survivors are the ones that have kept their costs-per-barrel low, either by being extra smart or lucky about where they choose to drill, or by relentlessly cutting costs. That's how the grow-or-die world of capitalism works.

Raising prices to cover the costs of careful, responsible production is also not an option. Oil is a commodity. Louisiana sweet crude sells on the international market for the same price per barrel no matter how it gets there. There's no premium for dolphin-safe crude. There's no organic gas. There's little incentive for companies to put extra care into their extraction methods. That's how commodities work. The market sets the price.

That's why the specialty coffee market was born. Coffee is the second-largest commodity product in the world, after oil. It, too, used to all sell for the same price, regardless of quality or production methods, meaning farmers' only incentive was to increase yield and cut costs. Hence all those decades of crappy coffee. But then, because both consumers and producers cared, an alternative "specialty" market arose, bypassing the commodity traders. Consumers paid significantly more per pound for delicious coffee, or organic coffee, or fair-trade coffee, in which farmers were guaranteed a living wage and pickers were guaranteed humane working conditions. Huge success.

Could something similar ever happen in the world of petroleum? Would you pay extra for gas that came from a rig that had two blind-shear rams on its blowout preventer? That used twenty-one stabilizers instead of six? That didn't dump its drilling fluids overboard? That always erred on the side of worker safety? That sent its oil to shore the long way, up the Mississippi, rather than carving new channels through the marshes? That was separated in a modern refinery that didn't leak benzene? That helped fund restoration efforts in the Gulf wetlands inevitably damaged by oil extraction?

I know I would. And I bet a lot of other people would, too. Still, bribing the most profitable corporations in history to take care of their workers and the environment would gall me. They can afford to do it—as long as all their rivals are forced to do it, too. And that means, yes, government.

Oil companies invest in safety all the time. They're no fools. They do it as long as that safety pays off in fewer fines, lawsuits, and so on. As long as it saves money. The higher the fines, the more punitive the lawsuits, the smarter an investment in safety becomes. Unfortunately, we as a society continue to do a terrible job of giving Big Oil any kind of safety incentive. The latest *wink, nudge* came from the Supreme Court, which reduced the punitive damages against Exxon for the 1989 *Exxon Valdez* oil spill from an original five billion dollars to a mere half billion. Since the accident, Exxon and other oil corporations have upgraded their tanker fleets to double hulls, but if they'd known how puny the penalty was going to be, I wonder if they'd have put it off. What happens with the fines and lawsuits for the *Deepwater Horizon* spill—which will also take years to wend their way through the courts—will go a long way toward determining how much emphasis Big Oil puts on safety in the future.

And this is where we're in danger of letting them off the hook. A veritable Mississippi of ink has been spilled on the subject of the *Deepwater Horizon* by dailies, magazines, and books, to say nothing of the electronic ink of the blogosphere. Much of that ink has been focused on the rig itself—what went wrong, what could have been done to prevent it, whose fault it was—or on BP's corporate culture and cost cutting. Yes, mistakes were made. Yes, BP cut corners. But to focus on that, rather than on the system that encouraged such decisions, is to miss the point in potentially dangerous ways.

To believe that the explosion was due to a few individual screwups is to play right into BP's hands. It wants you to believe that human error (*Transocean*'s and *Halliburton*'s human error, specifically) undermined its perfect plan. And to believe that the explosion was due to BP's corporate shortcuts is to play right into the hands of ExxonMobil, Shell, Chevron, and the rest of Big Oil. They want you to believe that, other than this cavalier corporation, oil extraction is a blameless business.

If we believe these things, then the focus becomes (as it has for Congress, always the most gullible of institutions) punishing the wrongdoers so it doesn't happen again. A very comforting feeling for us all. The criminals are removed from the system, justice is served, and the system thrives once again. The group cleanup efforts, the government as fall guy, the public flogging of CEOs—it all helps to convince us that the system works, so we'll feel better and won't change it.

Much less comforting—and certainly not something you'll hear any of Big Oil's CEOs stating before Congress—is the recognition that this is what happens when you have four thousand rigs operating in the Gulf, more and more of them at the edges of our know-how. This is what happens when you have twenty-seven thousand abandoned wells in the Gulf, many of them corroding. This is what happens when you have to tunnel five miles under the ocean in search of your resource. Human error cannot be expunged from the system when you have hundreds of thousands of people working with a highly flammable product under extraordinary pressure. The now-iconic images from the *Deepwater Horizon* spill—fireboats spraying their water cannons onto the flaming rig, shrimp boats corralling oil inside long strips of boom, blackened pelicans stepping over tar balls, coffins lowered into the ground in Texas and Louisiana—are what you get when Big Oil does ninety-nine out of one hundred things right. Yes, we should make sure it sinks almost every dollar of profit into safety, but even then, the occasional *oops* is unavoidable. This is what oops looks like. And no amount of teeth-gnashing or congressional investigations is going to prevent the next unthinkable oops, just as double-hulling tankers after the *Exxon Valdez* spill didn't prevent this disaster. Get ready for more frequent oopses in the future as the industry races to harvest the last great petroleum reserves from previously unthinkable places like the Arctic, the ultra-deep Brazilian coast, and Cuba, where the first wells will soon be drilled just sixty-five miles south of Key West with much less oversight than they would get in U.S. waters.

In the few months immediately after the *Deepwater Horizon*

explosion, a Mariner Energy rig caught fire in the Gulf of Mexico, endangering the lives of thirteen workers. A ruptured pipeline in Michigan spilled more than one million gallons of oil into the Kalamazoo River, contaminating a vast wetland. A natural gas pipeline exploded in San Bruno, California, killing six people and incinerating an entire neighborhood. This is what happens when you play with oil. Take it or leave it.

Chapter 12

CREATING LAND AND OTHER MINOR MIRACLES

STOP IN ANY welcome center in Louisiana and you'll discover handsome brochures created by a group called America's Wetland Foundation. "Time and Tide wait for no one," they read.

Since 1927, the leveeing of the Mississippi River has cut off fresh water, sediments and nutrients to the 7th largest delta on earth—a place called America's Wetland—causing coastal Louisiana to suffer. Every year, 24 miles of Louisiana shoreline washes away, resulting in the loss of valuable wetlands equal in size to a football field every 38 minutes. We are losing rapidly one of the most significant estuaries in the world, home to more than 70 rare, threatened and endangered species, and America's largest wintering habitat for migrating waterfowl and songbirds. Beyond world ecological significance, this is the heart of America's Energy Coast, a place where we fuel the nation, and provide for its domestic energy and economic security.

That last line does not sound like the work of your typical green group. But the waterfowl and marshes on the brochure sure make it look like the group's heart is in the right place. And page two makes so much sense: "Leading scientists and engineers have designed a solution to restore America's Wetland. The money for coastal protection and restoration does not need to come from the American taxpayer. Recently, Congress passed landmark legislation designed to support the rebuilding of coastal Louisiana through Outer Continental Shelf revenue sharing." This is explained in a bit more detail on the America's Wetland Foundation Web site: "Since its inception seven years ago, the AWF and its partners have called for a Federal commitment to environmental restoration of Louisiana's coast . . . AWF and many of its partners have been long-time advocates of the sharing of Federal offshore oil and gas revenues with the Gulf coast producing states to be used for coastal restoration and protection of this region."

To me, "a Federal commitment to environmental restoration" sure makes it sound like the money is coming from the American taxpayer. What's going on here? The primary funding for America's Wetland comes from Shell, though Chevron, ExxonMobil, Citgo, Dow Chemical, ConocoPhillips, and all the usual suspects contribute. Even BP kicks in. The *Huffington Post* calls America's Wetland a "front group" for the oil companies; America's Wetland claims that it's an attempt to bring all parties with a stake in wetlands restoration to the same table. Its partners include many of the leading green groups, including the Environmental Defense Fund, the National Wildlife Federation, the National Audubon Society, the Nature Conservancy, and Ducks Unlimited. That's right, when it comes to creating a restoration plan for the Gulf Coast, Chevron, ExxonMobil, BP, the Environmental Defense Fund, the National Wildlife Federation, and the Audubon Society are all working together!

Understanding what's going on here requires pulling back far enough that the usual blathering of both the oil companies and the greens can be put in context. As I've explained, the oil industry has ravaged the Gulf wetlands for a century, accounting for somewhere around half of the land losses with its drilling, dredging, and canal building. The oil companies denied that they were having an impact until the science became very, very obvious, at which point they became very, very fearful that they might someday be held accountable. The bill to restore the Gulf wetlands is currently estimated at a minimum of $100 billion; they certainly don't want to be on the hook for half of that.

So they switched tacks. Yes, this is "an ecosystem like no other, with majesty and beauty matched only by its mystery and diversity." Yes, it is "one of the most endangered places on earth." And whose fault is it? The Army Corps of Engineers, of course! If only they hadn't leveed the Mississippi! They should fix it. And who should pay? Well, since it was the government's fault, and since this is a landscape of "strategic importance to the nation's economic and energy security," America should pay. That's why the group is not called "Louisiana's Wetland"; this is America's problem.

Why would so many leading environmental organizations play ball? Well, one, because they are desperate for funding. And two, their usual tactics weren't getting anywhere—after decades of whining, they haven't achieved any substantial Gulf restoration. It's just too expensive. Numerous plans have been created for coastal restoration, always with hopelessly inadequate funding—a few million here, a few million there. The best effort Congress has been able to muster, called Coast 2050, would only manage to reduce the cumulative wetland losses by the year 2050 from five hundred thousand acres to four hundred thousand. Not exactly a solution.

So what did the greens have to lose by fraternizing with the oil companies, other than their souls, which were already pretty tattered. They called off their dogs. They still point to the damage caused in the past by the industry (to ignore it would be absurd), but they always call for federal funding.

The unsavory origins of America's Wetland hit the news in September 2010, when Sandra Bullock withdrew her support from a campaign created by a group called Women of the Storm, which has strong ties to America's Wetland. Not surprisingly, the video created by Women of the Storm called for the federal government to fund the restoration efforts. "Ms. Bullock was originally contacted through her attorney to be a part of the PSA [public service announcement] in order to promote awareness of the oil spill in the Gulf of Mexico," her publicist said. "At no time was she made aware that any organization, oil company or otherwise, had influence over Women of the Storm or its message. We have immediately asked for her participation in the PSA to be removed until the facts can be determined."

But Sandra Bullock aside, things are going well for America's Wetland, and for the oil industry as a whole, which received its greatest gift platter ever when BP managed to lose 205 million gallons of oil into the Gulf. For violating the rules of the Clean Water Act, BP must pay fines of at least $5 billion into the Oil Spill Liability Trust Fund, which was established to bankroll cleanup efforts for future oil spills. If BP is found to be grossly negligent, its fines could go as high as $21 billion. (When litigation is factored in, BP's total costs could exceed $60 billion.)

That's a big wad of cash. And in one of those rare and suspect displays of unity, everyone from the Environmental Defense Fund and the National Wildlife Federation to America's Wetland, not to mention every Gulf Coast politician, called for most of that money to be redirected to the Gulf states for restoration. The attraction for the Gulf states and politicians was obvious: Send us the $20 billion! Gulf senators and representatives had been after serious restoration pork for years, but they couldn't get their colleagues from the rest of the country interested in the cause. For the environmental groups, this was also a once-in-a-lifetime windfall; who cared where it was coming from? And for America's Wetland and the oil companies, what an opportunity: Instead of getting stuck with the bill for fixing the wetlands, they could stick BP with it! Even BP likes the idea—they're paying anyway; why not send the cash to their friends on the Gulf Coast, rather than to Washington, D.C.?

The only question is how much should go directly to the Gulf. Louisiana senator Mary Landrieu thinks it should be 80 percent (and has sponsored a bill to make that happen); the feds think maybe less (they can think of a few things they'd like to do with that cash). Whatever the final percentage, it should make large-scale restoration projects possible for the first time.

The devil will be in the details. On October 4, President Obama signed an executive order establishing the Gulf Coast Ecosystem Restoration Task Force, chaired by EPA administrator (and New Orleans native) Lisa Jackson. Good idea. But to the dismay of scientists everywhere, the task force was heavy on politicians and light on ecologists. It is made up of representatives from numerous federal agencies, everything from the EPA to the Departments of Defense and Commerce and Transportation, as well as representatives from each of the Gulf states. It will spend its first year coming up with a master plan—coordination between various parties, performance indicators for tracking progress, the whole Dilbert suite.

You know how that goes. A few billion dollars won't last long, especially if any coastal restoration actually occurs. Billions more is supposed to arrive a few years down the road, when the Natural Resources Damage Assessment and Restoration program completes its tally of how much BP must pay for every dead turtle, oiled oyster reef, and lost swimming day at the beach, but don't hold your breath. If BP pulls an Exxon, and drags the process through the courts as long as possible, it could take decades. (The process is only beginning for the eleven million gallons of oil spilled in 2005 during Hurricanes Katrina and Rita.) Beyond this, there's no serious plan to fund restoration once BP's penalty money runs out. Maybe the hope is that a major well blowout will come along every few years and replenish the fund?

Not long ago, there was real hope of more funding. On July 30, the House of Representatives passed the CLEAR Act, by a vote of 209–193, despite intense opposition from the energy industry. The bill imposed a two-dollar "conservation fee" on every barrel of oil produced in federal offshore waters. It would have provided about $1 billion per year in perpetuity purely for restoration. But in the Senate, Majority Leader Harry Reid buried the bill once it became clear how deadly it could be to vulnerable Democrats. Big help; after the midterm elections it was given up for dead. In fact, all spill bills seeking new taxes on oil died in the Senate once it became clear that Republicans and their oil industry masters were ascendant.

This is a shame, because we have a clear precedent: Just as tobacco companies must pay for the damage they do to American citizens, oil companies need to pay for the damage they do to American lands. This can be accomplished through untapped revenue sources that should be appealing to everyone, from greens to oil states. Currently, every barrel of oil produced in or imported into the United States is taxed 8 cents for the Oil Spill Liability Trust Fund. That brings in about $600 million per year, which has turned out to be rather inadequate for dealing with large spills. Eight cents is 0.1 percent of an $80 barrel of oil. It's a joke. And it doesn't accurately reflect the costs of oil production in ecological damage, climate change, human lives, and so on. Raise the tax to 13 cents per barrel, providing an even $1 billion per year for future spill cleanup costs. Then tack on 26 cents to generate $2 billion a year for Gulf restoration. That total tax—39 cents per 42-gallon barrel—is still less than a penny per gallon of oil. Meaningless in terms of both corporate profits and any increase we might see at the pump, but huge in terms of the life expectancy of the Gulf Coast.

Another appropriate funding source is the federal government's royalties from offshore oil leases, which averaged $2,224 per acre from 1954 to 1982, but dropped to a paltry $263 per acre between 1983 and 2008. Our own Government Accountability Office put it this way: "The U.S. federal government receives one of the lowest government takes in the world" on its oil resources. We have been giving away our offshore resources for nothing but the promise of a few jobs, offering "royalty holidays" and below-market royalty rates to encourage drilling that no longer needs encouraging. More than $50 billion in revenue— enough to power a full-blown restoration of the Gulf Coast—has been waived. The U.S. receives a total "government take"— which includes royalties, lease auctions, and taxes collected—on its deepwater oil of about 40 percent, which came in thirtieth out of thirty-one governments studied by Louisiana State University. (Only Mexico, at 31 percent, was lower. The U.K.'s take is 52 percent, Australia's about 54 percent, Egypt's 61 percent, and Norway's 76 percent.) If we're going to let these multinational corporations have our oil—oil we will desperately need in the future—let's at least get decently compensated for it.

These royalties have simply gone to the Treasury, but the 2007 Gulf of Mexico Energy Security Act calls for Louisiana to begin receiving 35.7 percent of the revenue from offshore Gulf leases—which should add up to about $500 million per year—starting in 2017. The Gulf states would love to speed up that transition. I agree—so long as the revenue goes to fix the damage caused by oil extraction.

That's a long shot, I know. Such money has a way of disappearing into tax cuts and other sweeteners, rather than funding any long-term projects. At the very least, a big chunk of BP penalty money is going to arrive for restoration in the next few years—a hundred times what's ever been available before. When it does, we'd better have a pretty good idea how we want it spent; otherwise, we leave it to the amorphous federal task force and state politicians. A few suggestions:

- **Don't spend it all at once.** No Congress in the immediate future is going to have the combination of power and foresight needed to create any sort of perpetual revenue source for Gulf restoration, or any other sort of conservation. BP is going to be our only involuntary philanthropist. Whatever Clean Water Act penalties it pays will have to serve as the endowment for Gulf restoration. Put it in a fund, and issue the interest as annual grants to nonprofits, universities, and local agencies on a competitive basis.

- **Focus on diversions first.** Until we reverse the land-subsidence trends in the Mississippi River Delta, other restoration work is futile. Land must be created. Serious, large-scale freshwater diversions need to be built into the Mississippi levee system. This won't be easy. Thanks to the scores of major dams on the Missouri and Mississippi rivers, most river sediment now settles to the bottom of reservoirs instead of reaching the Mississippi River Delta. There may no longer be enough sediment to create significant new land, as the Mississippi did for seven thousand years. But there is enough to stop the losses and to protect what we still have.

- **Use dredged sediment.** When the water in the Mississippi River hits the Gulf of Mexico, it slows down and silts up. The mouth of the river needs to be constantly dredged to remain navigable. Every year, twenty-two million cubic yards of sediment are scooped out of the river and dumped into deep water off the continental shelf because official Army Corps of Engineers policy states that the sediment must be disposed of "in the least costly manner." This policy needs to change, ASAP, so that all this brown gold can be used to make new marshes and fill inactive canals.

- **Get the Midwest to do its part.** The Gulf will never recover as long as the pig farms, chicken factories, cornfields, and septic systems of half of America continue to dump mountains of nitrogen and phosphorus into it. The dead zone must die, and that means major upgrades of sewage treatment plants, a switch to no-till farming (which dramatically reduces runoff), a rejection of chemical fertilizer (the source of most of that nitrogen), and much higher standards of cleanliness and manure control in industrial agriculture.

- **Make it a working wetland.** Ultimately, Gulf restoration will only become a part of life on the Gulf Coast if the wetlands become, once again, a part of people's lives. Livings once were made from those marshes and beaches, and they can be again. The same skills needed to service the offshore rigs and platforms—boat handling, construction, engineering, backhoe and crane operation, and support—are needed for major wetlands-restoration efforts. When many Gulf Coasters' jobs are involved in restoration, the project will seem as vital as the project to pump oil out of the ground.

- **Get everyone involved.** A portion of the endowment should go toward letting the rest of the country in on the secret of this extraordinary environment. Gulf Coast tourism officials worry about restoring their industry to what it was before the spill, but the larger truth is that the region's tourism has never lived up to its potential, because the "Oil Coast" manages to terrify a fair number of East Coasters, West Coasters, and foreigners. When the Gulf Coast is where America and the world come to swim, fish, paddle, dive, stroll, dance, and eat, it won't be allowed to turn into Nigeria anymore.

- **Spread it out.** Gulf restoration must mean more than just the Mississippi River Delta. It means restoring oyster reefs from Texas to Florida. It means nurturing places like Grand Bay. It means making the entire Gulf Coast a vibrant, resilient place. "If I'm going to spend the next ten years doing this," Bill Finch said, "I want to make sure that the next time something like this happens, this place has as much resilience as it can to withstand these onslaughts, including climate change and hurricanes and everything else. We need more space for these habitats to move, as they've always done. We can't say, 'I'm going to buy this habitat and put a fence around it.' Something may happen to that particular piece. All these ecosystems need redundancy. I'll work ten years on this if I can see that we're actually taking this seriously now. It would make me feel *good* to work on it if we can actually gain some ground."

It would make us all feel good. It's hard to put a price on what feeling good is worth, but many a clinically depressed person will assure you that they'd pay everything they have for the opportunity. Think about the national depression that sunk in after the *Deepwater Horizon* spill, then think about what it would feel like to know that the greatest wetland in the world had not only been saved from oblivion but was also actually getting better—healthier, cleaner, more full of life and beauty and livelihoods.

Chapter 13

THE MOST IMPORTANT RIVER
YOU'VE NEVER HEARD OF

B ACK IN MAY, when I stood with Wendy Billiot near the
Houma Nav and stared at acre upon acre of bleached, dead
cypress trunks, my overwhelming emotion was neither anger
nor sadness but desire: Seeing a dead cypress swamp gave me a
compelling need to experience a live one. Otherwise, I risked
becoming part of the national shifting baseline. It's hard to care
too deeply for something you've never known.

At the time, I'd thought I'd head for the Atchafalaya swamp.
The Atchafalaya River—the one that has been trying to capture the Mississippi for the better part of a century—remains
somewhat free. Instead of corseting the river right along its
banks, as was done on the Mississippi, the Army Corps of Engineers built the Atchafalaya's levees about fifteen miles apart,
leaving a natural spillway that starts 315 miles upriver from the
mouth of the Mississippi and runs about 150 miles straight south
to the Gulf. No one is allowed to live in this 833,000-acre basin, because it is where, in times of catastrophic flood, the Corps
sends the excess Mississippi. The rest of the time, the Old River
Control Structure ensures that exactly 30 percent of the flow of

the Mississippi diverts into the Atchafalaya River. Famously, because the Atchafalaya has been allowed to flood, its delta has continued to expand—within the confines of the levees. It's the poster swamp for wetlands advocates, a justly celebrated sportsman's paradise of swamp, crawfish, and waterfowl.

Yet no one lives there, and the entire basin is fed through the concrete gates of the Old River Control Structure, so it wasn't quite what I was looking for. I wanted an old-school swamp, peopled and free. And I was lucky enough to find it.

I'd heard about a guy named Don Abrams, an engineer who lived in Ocean Springs, Mississippi, and who, in the days after the spill, had pulled together a list of seven thousand volunteers eager to help protect the coast from the oil. He'd set up an entire Web site devoted to it. And he'd been unable to find anyone at BP or the Coast Guard willing to even take a look at the list.

When I called Don, it turned out that he was also the volunteer at the Gulf Coast Research Laboratory who was taking Jimbo Meador's SWAT boat into the marshes, documenting oiled zones. I tagged along. Right in Biloxi Bay, on Marsh Point, Don showed me some sickening oil damage. A stretch of cordgrass was so thickly matted in gooey tar that it had no hope of recovery. If you touched it, your fingers stuck together. Somehow this blot of oil had slipped through the nets of hundreds of Vessels of Opportunity patrolling Mississippi's sixty-two miles of coastline. The absorbent boom that was supposed to be the next line of defense was sprawled on top of the marsh grass, balled up in the oil. Beside it lay a blackened, burned-out hunk of high-tech foam, possibly wreckage from the *Deepwater Horizon*. Don had reported the wreckage to BP, but somehow it was still here. He'd seen a ten-person cleanup crew visit the island a few days after the oil arrived on May 10. They set up a tent and stayed about a week. "Most of the time they sat in the shade," Don said. "Once I saw them with paper towels, trying to wipe the oil off the grass. Another time they tried blasting it with saltwater." Eventually they gave up and left. When we were out there, they had been replaced by an amphibious trackhoe parked on the bank. Its crew sat in the shade.

Don is a deeply committed fly fisherman, and the spill had hit him hard. Several weeks a year he boats out to the Chandeleur Islands, the fabled fifty-mile crescent of barrier islands between the Louisiana and Mississippi coasts that is the remnant of the Mississippi River Delta of two thousand years ago. He stays on a floating fish camp and communes all day with one of the world's great fishing spots. "The inside coast of the islands is an enormous bank, mostly less than four feet deep," Don told me. "It's just these stunning meadowlands. Like Kansas underwater. Unbelievably productive stuff. All kinds of fish live there. Grouper, amberjack, speckled trout, redfish, mackerel, cobia. And that seagrass is very susceptible to oil." The Chandeleurs were the first land to be hit by the oil spill, and they had suffered three different waves of oil. Don's friend who operates the fish camp was depressed. "He said the odor was awful. He could taste it. He had a constant headache."

If you stepped onto the Chandeleurs today, you wouldn't think you were in underwater Kansas anymore. That's because after the spill, Governor Bobby Jindal jumped on a harebrained scheme to block the incoming oil by building a wall of sand berms off the coast, funded by $360 million from BP. Although the plan was decried by virtually every scientist on the coast, the scheme accomplished its task, which was to make Jindal popular with voters, who loved his act-first-and-ask-questions-later approach, and with the construction and engineering firms that got the bids for the project, at least one of which was a major campaign contributor. Heavy machinery descended on the Chandeleurs, which are a part of Breton National Wildlife Refuge, and miles of underwater sandy habitat were dredged—killing endangered sea turtles in the process—and blasted onto the low-lying islands to connect them. Even months after the Macondo well had been capped, the oil had dispersed, and the berms had proved completely ineffective, the dredging went on.

Don told me he couldn't bear to visit the Chandeleurs now, even places that looked clean. Just the thought of what was happening took all the fun out of it. To me, that's an important point. We don't interact with the coast—whether it's fishing, swimming, or just exploring—simply for seafood or exercise or entertainment. We look to immerse ourselves in a place that is alive and sustaining, to take pleasure in its vitality. If the place is suffering, then the magic is gone.

Instead of the coast, Don suggested that we get our nature fix a few miles north, in the Pascagoula River Swamp. And he knew just the guy to take us there. Don had a friend who had a daughter who worked at the only paddling company in Ocean Springs, and she was dating a twenty-two-year-old swamp dude named Gene Cossey. Gene's people all live near the swamp, and from the time he could walk, he'd been eating things in it: bass, mullet, gar, redfish, crappie, speckled trout, crawfish, frog, duck, deer, boar, nutria, beaver. Gene has smoked a beaver or two, which he says is "pretty good, still gamy," but recently, in a moment of desperation, he'd stir-fried a beaver in a Szechuan sauce and pronounced the results "awesome." I will not try to reproduce Gene's accent in type. He sounds like a hunk of that beaver is still stuck in his cheek.

Gene, known locally as the "Renaissance Bubba" because of his wide-ranging talents, is an organic gardener, a kayak guide, a mechanic. He'd recently modified a gas burner so that it could bring five gallons of water to a boil in three minutes, the better to boil vast quantities of peanuts. It sounded like a jet engine. He lives with his grandmother and takes care of her.

Gene agreed to show us the swamp. We met him at the kayak shop, piled in his truck, and drove north through pine woods, the roads getting progressively smaller. At one clearing, Gene said idly, "That's where I shot my first buck." Later, as we crossed a tiny bridge, "That there creek has the coldest water in the county. It's great for bream." What was undifferentiated South to me was, to him, a landscape textured with memory and meaning.

We put in our kayaks at a place called Poticaw Bayou and slipped beneath a canopy of oak, sweet gum, and swamp maple on blackwater curls. Rotting houseboats serving as floating fishing camps—some weekend getaways, some full-time residences— dotted the bayous. They were decorated with antlers and fishing poles. Sagging rocking chairs sat on the porches. It was pure *Deliverance*, enough to confirm all of your Mississippi stereotypes, though Gene won't. Sure, he shoots the occasional hog with his .243 and talks funny, but he also loves international cooking and was a cross-country champion in high school. He's got the build of a Kenyan marathoner—small, wiry, no excess. Black hair, black beard, strong as an ant. After high school he knocked around doing concrete and construction work for a few years before hooking up with his kayaking girlfriend. Now he leads a lot of the paddling company's tours. "I wish more people wanted to come up here," he said. Gene said the Pascagoula hasn't changed since he was a kid, though pretty much every other place he knows has.

The largest free-flowing river in the Lower 48, the Pascagoula is the most important river you've never heard of, a perfect example of the Gulf Coast's inferiority complex. Its forests
have all the jungly, broad-leafed complexity and species rich-
ness of the tropical rainforest, and even more aquatic diversity,
yet every year millions of us fly over it on our way to Belize or
Costa Rica. Anywhere else, it would be famous. Instead, America
leaves it to the locals and the gators.

The blackwater bayous of the Pascagoula River Swamp weave
together through ten thousand square miles of wilderness, their
currents virtually undetectable until they join the main channel
of the Pascagoula River. Without Gene, I'd have been instantly
lost amid the tangle of side creeks that slip through the forest. At
least 109 species of fish have been found in the Pascagoula, including endangered ones like the gulf sturgeon, which can reach two
hundred pounds and has been nosing through these rivers for
sixty-three million years, swimming many miles upstream to
spawn. Hundreds of bird species, both full-timers and migrants,
depend on it. Ivory-billed woodpeckers and panthers are still ru-
mored to haunt it. It's thick with otters and bears and turtles
found nowhere else. Why the Pascagoula was never dammed,
leveed, or dredged is a quirk of history, but its ultimate preservation came through an unprecedented coalition of hunting, fishing, and environmental groups in the 1970s. Today, fifty of the
river's eighty-one miles are preserved.

Yet it is far from safe. A few years ago, the Bush administration's Department of Energy decided the area would make the
ideal spot for an expansion of the Strategic Petroleum Reserve.
For five years, subterranean salt domes north of the river would
be dissolved, using fifty million gallons *per day* of river water,
and filled with 160 million barrels of crude, piped in from tanks

on the Gulf Coast, to be saved for a national emergency. Not only will heavy machinery tear through the Pascagoula, laying pipe, but also the river itself will be substantially lowered, cutting off the swamp from its water and nutrients. Meanwhile, the salt-blasting process will create forty-two million gallons of toxic brine every day. In theory, this will all get piped through the swamp to the Gulf near the west end of Petit Bois Island, where it will disperse into the Gulf. But the cookie-cutter environmental-impact statements for the project didn't even take tides into account.

Even the Department of Energy itself estimates that seventy-five brine leaks will occur during the life of the project, poisoning various spots on the Pascagoula. This is in addition to the estimated eighteen oil spills that will pour into the area as oil is pumped from coastal terminals, through the watershed, to the underground storage caverns. Then there is the question of whether any of that oil sitting beneath the surface will escape. The powers that be, you may not be surprised to hear, assure us that they will take every safety precaution, that the possibility of a leak is . . . unthinkable.

Days before the *Deepwater Horizon* explosion, the Obama administration pulled the funding for the seventy-one-million-dollar project, citing budget shortfalls, but it is a favorite of Mississippi senator Thad Cochran, and it lives on, as unkillable as oil itself, biding its time, waiting to be unearthed once the proper stars align in Congress and the White House.

What a devastating loss that will be. Mississippi Wildlife Federation board member Justin Sward said, "The Pascagoula can teach you anything you want to know if you just sit there and listen." Hundreds, possibly thousands of archaeological sites dot the swamp. American Indians found it an ideal place to live, just as Gene does today. The absence of dams or levees allows all the system's energies to flow freely. Fish move upstream; floods deposit nutrients throughout the forested bottomlands; thousand-year-old cypress slowly die and nurture new generations of insects and fungi, instead of being hauled off to the mill.

As we paddled a couple of miles downstream, the land dropped low enough that the oaks and swamp maple couldn't hack it. Only the water tupelo and bald cypress held on, sticking their skeletal selves out of the marsh grass, platforms for osprey nests. Knobby cypress knees, which provide stability in the mud and draw oxygen into the roots, crowded the banks. Green herons croaked out of our way. The water seethed with baitfish. Golden light slanted through the canopy and caught the occasional gator or gar silently submerging as we passed. Gene's songline-like narration continued. "Last year we tore it up on bass in that cove right there." There's something about cypress swamps—something archetypal about gliding past living trees emerging from the water, ducking thatches of artichoke-gray Spanish moss, gazing through the ranks of shady silhouettes—that tugs at your inner hunter-gatherer.

The river widened. The trees gave way to reed-lined banks. No shade. It was only ten A.M., but this was Mississippi in summer. Sweat beaded down my chest. A Spanish mackerel, a superb saltwater game fish, leaped out of the water. Gene frowned. "Don't usually see them up here," he said. "Been seein' a lot more deepwater fish since the spill."

A beautiful sandbar opened up on a bend in the river. We beached our kayaks and swam in the soft, tan water. Crabs shadowboxed our toes. Behind the sandbar, a scrim of rushes screened a pool from the main river. "Look at those bull minnows!" said Gene. "I gotta remember to come here for bait fish."

Farther still, we paddled under I-10 and the river opened up into the Pascagoula Delta, an infinitude of salt marsh. In the distance we could see rigs and cranes like skyscrapers. The Pascagoula shoreline is dominated by the oil industry, and the river was feeding us right into it, a sort of *Farewell to Shady Glade* in reverse. We climbed back in our kayaks and made our way to the haul-out spot. I thanked Gene for showing us his swamp. He said sure. Then he asked if we wanted to go frog gigging that night.

Well, *of course.* Don had told me that Gene's char-grilled frog legs were to die for.

At dusk, with the temperature threatening to drop below ninety and the mosquitoes testing liftoff, we rendezvoused with Gene at a broken-down convenience store at the edge of the swamp, tossed our gear into a skiff on a trailer behind his truck, and made our way down increasingly rutted sand roads. Twice we caught a flash of the violet glow of a blacklight deep in the forest. I thought maybe we should investigate. Gene thought maybe we shouldn't. "Some people around here you don't want to meet."

Finally we stopped at a boat launch in serious disrepair. The bottom of it had crumbled in a muddy mess, but it was good enough to unload a skiff. We stepped out of the truck and let the warm, wet air encircle us. A deafening, clackety sound wuffled my eardrums. "What's that sound?" I asked.

"What sound?" said Gene.

"That deafening, clackety sound," I said.

"Oh, *that.* Cicadas."

From the boat launch, a small, crescent-shaped lake opened up. Like all lakes in the Pascagoula swamp, it was once an ox-bow in the river that was eventually cut off and bypassed. Now it was quiet and stagnant, cypress trees protruding from its shorelines like buttressed columns in an ancient, flooded temple.

To gig frogs, you creep along the edge of a lake at night, shin-
ing a spotlight along the shoreline, where the bullfrogs like to
hang out, croaking their deep mating calls into the dark. When
you catch a frog in the spotlight, it freezes, allowing you to get
close. As long as it doesn't catch a glimpse of your shadow, it will
stay put. One of us would crouch in the bow of the skiff with the
gig, a ten-foot metal pole with three flexible prongs at the end
that spear the frog. Then you bring it back to the boat and dis-
patch it with a knife. The other would stand just behind with the
light, while the third would pole us along. You get within gigging distance, then let fly and try to impale the frog.

We poled the skiff through moss-draped cypress trunks,
breaking through endless spiderwebs, moon and stars caught below us in the black mirror of water. Occasional fish stirred the
surface, and alligators' red eyes reflected in our light, submerging
as we approached. Tree frogs trilled in the ferns. The air was
dead still, thick with honeysuckle. *Croak, croak* went the banks.

The others were flawless frog giggers. Then it was my turn.
I squatted in the bow with my right arm pulled back like Que-
equeg on the *Pequod*. Don froze a frog in the spotlight. It was
the size of a goddamn chicken. But I must have twitched as we
approached, because it suddenly turned, hopped a few feet up
the steep bank, and turned back to watch us. It was now about
six feet up the bank, looking straight at us. I was zoning in on
it in a sort of autistic fugue state and didn't think about the implications of its position. To reach it, I stepped off the bow into
the shore muck, moving in slow motion. At last, I was within
range. I waited, took a breath, and let fly—way, way too slow.
The tip of my gig thwacked into the bank as the frog launched
itself straight at my head, its eyes glowing huge in the spotlight.
I let out a yelp the likes of which I'm sure had never before been

heard in the Pascagoula River Swamp, the frog soared past my ear and into the water, and the cicadas were suddenly drowned out by the sound of uncontrollable male laughter. After that, I never got a good shot at a frog. But that was okay. Honestly, all I cared about was being in that sweet place, listening to the sounds. It felt like Dagobah. I expected Yoda to come tottering out of his mud hut. I wanted to stay all night. I'd never been anywhere so supple and layered with life.

How long it will be there, I don't know. The stars may again be aligning for the Strategic Petroleum Reserve. We may stop it for a year or two, but can we really stop it forever? So I'd say, if you want to experience the free-flowing, ecologically complete Gulf Coast, go now. Start in the Pascagoula's bottomland forest and cypress swamp, then drift down to the freshwater marshes, then the salt marsh, then let the river take you out into the Gulf and the seagrass meadows. Go now. And take pictures for your grandkids, so they'll believe you when you tell them how good it was.

Epilogue

THANKSGIVING

A S THE SUMMER of the Slick slid toward the Autumn
After, the Gulf Coast did its best to recover from its trauma
and move on. A thousand VOOs still plied the waters, scooping
up the odd patch of oil, but most of the coast was trying hard to
regain some sense of normalcy. The people I'd spent time with
on the Gulf over the summer were having mixed success with
that.

Wendy Billiot was trying to hang on to her eco-tour business.
She'd been asked by the StoryCorps project to discuss how the
spill had affected her. Typically, she'd risen to the task. "In spite
of the damage caused by the oil spill," she said, "in spite of the
worry about how far-reaching the effects of the dispersants might
be, it's made me want to take people out even more, to see the
beauty here. I've realized how precarious our lives are here on
the Gulf Coast. We have to look at what we have; we have to
appreciate what we have. We have to respect the bounty. We
have to conserve it—while enjoying it. Because something like a
failed blowout preventer can change all of it in an instant. It
could just be gone."

Josh Deupree had been sailing a lot, and winning a lot. "It's pretty cool, because we've been the underdog for so long," he told me. He'd been focusing his energies on teaching kids to sail, hoping to recruit a junior team for next year's races. "Most people haven't been talking about the oil much," he said. "I just try not to think about it much. Everyone is concerned about the long-term effects on the seafood, but we're all eating it. I guess if we all get sick in a few years, there will be another story."

Kadoo was eating shrimp again, too, buying it from his neighbors. "So far, I didn't get sick," he said. "We're gonna take it like it is, make the best of it." It was mid-November, and he was chatting with me on his cell phone as he stood in his back-yard, burning a pile of plastic bags, bottles, and wooden two-by-twos that had been left behind by the cleanup crews. "I warned 'em! Said I was gonna burn it if they left it. Got to make the place look nice, ya know. Nuttin' bad. No big deal. Might as well burn it."

As he'd predicted during the summer, Kadoo had stuck with the spill-response work, traveling up to Michigan with his crew—driving eighteen hours, straight through—to clean up the oil spill on the Kalamazoo River. "To be honest, I never did get on the river," he admitted. As in Louisiana, the responsible parties tried to hire locals for the cleanup, so Kadoo's crew stood around on standby for a week, cashed their checks, then drove back to Louisiana.

By the end of September, BP had closed the cleanup operation in Pointe-aux-Chenes, and Kadoo was out of work once again. By November, he was getting ready to head back out to the oys-ter reefs of Terrebonne Parish. Prices were pretty good—twenty-five dollars per sack—and unlike the reefs closer to the river and the diversions, the ones around him were in decent shape. "We seen some oil," he said. "Nuttin' to get excited over. Only thing that's gonna hurt us is that chemical. Long run, that might really hurt us."

Those Terrebonne oysters were some of the only ones Al Sunseri was able to find in Louisiana for P&J Oysters. Overall, he estimated that the state's harvest was about 14 percent of normal, and most of those were coming from the western part of the state. In his traditional areas near the Mississippi, harvest had been "less than 1 percent." P&J hadn't shucked an oyster since June 10, though Al and his brother were still sourcing some oysters from Texas and Alabama and delivering them in the shell to a handful of longtime clients. He hoped to gear up and rehire his shuckers in 2011, but he wasn't sure how many customers he'd have. "Our customers have been really loyal, but we haven't had oysters, so they've had to look elsewhere. These are people who never would have considered looking elsewhere." He wasn't having any luck getting BP to cover his losses. "They threw a few dollars at us early on, mainly to keep us quiet. Their MO is PR."

When I spoke with Al, it was just a few days before Thanksgiving. One of the great French Quarter traditions is the oyster spread P&J puts out between Thanksgiving and Christmas. They open up a walk-in retail business, and families from throughout the city come to try different oysters and oyster dishes and buy their holiday supplies. "I've got grown adults who have been coming since they were ten-year-old kids," he said. This year, for the first time ever, there would be no spread.

Mississippi's Don Abrams had ventured out to the Chandeleur Islands twice in October. "It's like an industrial site," he told me. "Two dormitory structures for workers, three enormous dredges, hundreds of workers, and dozens of workboats. Jindal's sand berm now stretches five miles or so and they're still building.

One good blow and the berm is going to melt." Meanwhile, tons of tar balls were being removed from the barrier islands every day, with no end in sight. "I was there about two weeks ago with a fellow from the lab, and we were unable to distinguish between the areas that had been cleaned and those that had not. Once again we were hassled by the hired security people, who went ballistic when we brought the cameras out." The cleanup crews went home for Thanksgiving, so Don took advantage of the momentary peacefulness and spent the weekend on Mississippi's Cat Island, catching redfish by kayak up in the marshes.

Unlike those I spoke with in Louisiana, Don felt that the spill had changed coastal Mississippians' attitudes toward the oil industry and its government cronies. "Most of us are disgusted with the way the response is being handled. We feel betrayed. We feel like we've not received good information. There's a general feeling that BP is getting away with something horrible, and they're able to do it only by virtue of spreading money around and having lots of friends in government."

Bill Finch chose to do an all-Gulf-seafood Thanksgiving: boiled crab, fried shrimp, oysters on the half shell. As he explained in a special Thanksgiving Day editorial in the *Mobile Press-Register*, "as the spill spread, I resolved I would not miss a sacred opportunity to savor and say thanks for the bounty of the Gulf, if there was anything left to be thankful for when the spill was over." For those who felt safer with the traditional entrée, he had this to say: "The modern turkey industry is built on the bounty of the Gulf of Mexico." In particular, it depends on Gulf menhaden just like those we had heard skipping around our sailboat at dusk. "And all of those who are thankful this Thanksgiving that they're not eating fish from the Gulf of

Mexico will want to be aware of this key stat: The two primary consumers of Gulf of Mexico fishmeal are chickens and turkeys. Yes, your butterball of a Thanksgiving turkey was brought to you at great cost to the Gulf of Mexico, and it's likely that the juicy white breast already harbors the impacts of this year's oil spill. Next year's turkey, not to mention your chicken pot pies and chicken nuggets, will be even more deeply imprinted with the spill's impacts."

Bill had left the Nature Conservancy to take not one but two jobs. He was director of the Mobile Botanical Gardens, perfect for a plant guy like Bill. He was eagerly moving forward on "a lot of great plans for educational programs that will help folks learn more about the sacredness of where they are." He'd also been named a senior fellow by the Ocean Foundation, whose motto is "Tell us what you want to do for the ocean. We will take care of the rest," which seemed pretty timely to me. There, he was working on a project called the 100-1000: Restore Coastal Alabama Partnership with the Nature Conservancy, the Alabama Coastal Foundation, and Mobile Baykeeper, among other groups. The coalition is raising funds and creating a team to rebuild a hundred miles of oyster reef and a thousand miles of marsh in Mobile Bay in the next few years.

"In Mobile Bay we're down to 10 percent of the grass beds, 10 percent of the marshes, 10 percent of the oyster reefs from what we had a hundred years ago," Bill says in a video produced by the coalition. And those numbers were from before the spill. "Every egg, every fish, every turtle, every young shrimp is precious now. Those are the two-by-two creatures that we're going to have to load into this ark of recovery we're building. We're going to need a place for these creatures to come home to. And we've got to restore the habitats that we've lost . . . We know how to do it! In Mobile Bay, we can rebuild a hundred miles of oyster reefs. We can rebuild at least a thousand acres of marsh and seagrass. In three to five years! Huge new areas of clean habitat for these creatures to come home to . . . If we do this, if we act heroically right now, in ten years we'll be living with a Gulf that is more bountiful—more beautiful!—than the Gulf we lived with before the spill came."

ACKNOWLEDGMENTS

I had just wrapped up some writing projects in April 2010 when the *Deepwater Horizon* exploded and the Macondo well began spewing oil into the Gulf. The story touched on a lot of subjects close to my heart—I'd written books about both oysters and the importance of estuaries, and I'd read everything there was to read on Peak Oil—and so I found myself obsessively reading about the disaster every day. For more than a week, I delved deeper and deeper into the subject while worrying about not working. Then Jeremy Spencer, my editor at *Outside*, asked me if I wanted to go down there and check it out. Did I! Without Jeremy, who published my "Sailing the Slick" chapter in the magazine in different form, I might never have put two and two together.

While visiting the Gulf region, I benefited hugely from the knowledge, insights, and generosity of many people. In particular, Alabama's Bill Finch and Mississippi's Don Abrams went out of their way to introduce me to the nature and culture of their homes and to make me feel welcome. This book is much better for their input, and I look forward to learning more from both of them for years to come. Wendy Billiot, Jimbo Meador, Josh Deupree, Jeff Dequattro, Judy Haner, Virgil Dardar, Al Sunseri, Leanne Sarco, and Gene Cossey all spent hours speaking with me, which greatly enriched the book. Thanks to the numerous scientists, cleanup workers, fishermen, and other Gulf Coasters I talked to whose names I never learned. Thanks to Ed Cake and Rebecca Cole for the steady stream of articles and links. Thanks to Ellen Miller for the speckled trout, Cecil Gardner for the sailboat, Andy Anderson for the photos, and Reese Hersey for the thoughts on "place and placelessness." The writings of hundreds of authors and journalists, past and present, informed my understanding of the region, its history, and this crisis, but the following were particularly vital: Oliver Houck, John McPhee, Ben Raines, Mike Tidwell, and Julia Whitty.

In New York, my agent Russ Galen's enthusiasm for the project, right from the beginning, was contagious, and my editor Kathy Belden's advocacy was key. Copyeditor Maureen Klier has pulled off the remarkable task of making this and my previous books seem as if they had sprung from a contiguous mind. Thanks to Mary and Eric for letting me work weekends. Writing a book on an urgent, fast-developing subject, and getting it out fast, is rough. Couldn't have done it without this whole team.

SOURCES

Chapter 2: THE LAST HUNTER-GATHERERS IN AMERICA

Carrier, Jim. "All You Can Eat." *Orion*, March–April 2009.
DeSantis, John. "Oil Hits Local Islands." *Houma Courier*, May 13, 2010.

Chapter 3: HOW GOOD IT WAS

Jacobsen, Rowan. *The Living Shore*. New York: Bloomsbury, 2009.
Montgomery, David. *Dirt*. Berkeley: University of California Press, 2008.

Chapter 4: THE BLACKEST SAUCE

Bower, Tom. "Drilling Down: A Troubled Legacy in Oil." *Wall Street Journal*, May 1–2, 2010.
Broad, William. "Tracing Oil Reserves to Their Tiny Origins." *New York Times*, August 3, 2010.
Hoffman, Carl. "Onboard High-Tech Oil Rig, U.S. Answers to Rising Prices." *Popular Mechanics*, October 1, 2009.
King, Neil, and Keith Johnson. "An Oil-Thirsty America Barreled into 'Dead Sea.'" *Wall Street Journal*, October 8, 2010.
Klare, Michael. "A New Oil Rush Endangers the Gulf of Mexico and the Planet." Tomdispatch.com, May 18, 2010. http://www

.tomdispatch.com/post/175249/tomgram%3A_michael_klare
,_the_oil_rush_to_hell.

Leopold, Jason. "Whistleblower: BP Risks More Massive Catastrophes in Gulf." Truthout, April 30, 2010. http://www.truth-out
.org/whistlelower-bps-other-offshore-drilling-project-gulf
-vulnerable-catastrophe59027.

Mouawad, Jad. "Drilling Deep in the Gulf of Mexico." *New York Times*, November 8, 2006.

——. "For BP, a History of Spills and Safety Lapses." *New York Times*, May 8, 2010.

Mouawad, Jad, and Barry Meier. "Risk-Taking Rises as Oil Rigs in Gulf Drill Deeper." *New York Times*, August 29, 2010.

Urbina, Ian. "U.S. Said to Allow Drilling Without Needed Permits." *New York Times*, May 13, 2010.

U.S. Energy Information Administration. *Performance Profiles of Major Energy Producers 2008*. December 2009. http://www.eia.doe
.gov/emeu/perfpro.

Voosen, Paul. "Gulf of Mexico's Deepwater Oil Industry Is Built on Pillars of Salt." *New York Times*, July 28, 2010.

Weber, Harry, and John Flesher. "World's Oil Thirst Leads to Risks." *Houma Courier*, November 5, 2010.

Whaley, Jane. "Huge Potential Still Waiting in Gulf of Mexico." *Geo ExPro*, September 2006.

Chapter 5: "The Unthinkable Has Become Thinkable"

Achenbach, Joel. "At BP, Safety vs. Cost-Saving." *Washington Post*, October 9, 2010.

Associated Press. "Gulf Oil Spill: Anatomy of a Disaster." CBS News, September 9, 2010.

Barstow, David, et al. "Lapses Found in Oversight of Failsafe Device on Oil Rig." *New York Times*, June 20, 2010.

Berman, Arthur E. "Causes and Implications of the BP Gulf of Mexico Oil Spill." Association for the Study of Peak Oil–USA World Oil Conference, October 9, 2010.

BP. *Deepwater Horizon Accident Investigation Report.* September 8, 2010. http:// www.bp.com/ . . . /Deepwater_Horizon_Accident_Investigation_Report.pdf.

Broder, John. "Firms Knew of Cement Flaws Before Spill, Panel Says." *New York Times*, October 28, 2010.

Bustillo, Miguel. "Big Spat on Rig Preceded Explosion." *Wall Street Journal*, May 27, 2010.

Casselman, Ben. "Rig Workers Had Chance to Prevent Explosion." *Wall Street Journal*, September 11, 2010.

Casselman, Ben, and Russ Gold. "Unusual Decisions Set Stage for BP Disaster." *Wall Street Journal*, May 27, 2010.

Deepwater Horizon Joint Investigation. (http://www.deepwaterinvestigation.com/go/site/3043/) Testimony of Douglas Brown, May 26, 2010.

———. Testimony of Nathaniel Chaisson, August 24, 2010.

———. Testimony of Jesse Gagliano, August 24, 2010.

———. Testimony of John Guide, October 7, 2010.

———. Testimony of Jimmy Harrell, May 27, 2010.

———. Testimony of Christopher Pleasant, May 28, 2010.

———. Testimony of Vincent Tabler, August 25, 2010.

———. Testimony of Greg Walz, October 7, 2010.

Gillis, Justin. "Estimates of Oil Flow Jump Higher." *New York Times*, June 15, 2010.

Gold, Russell, and Ben Casselman. "On Doomed Rig's Last Day, a Divisive Change of Plan." *Wall Street Journal*, August 26, 2010.

Halliburton. "Halliburton Comments on National Commission Cement Testing." Press release, October 28, 2010.

Hammer, David. "BP Engineer Defends Decision to Reject Oil Well Safety Advice." *New Orleans Times-Picayune*, October 7, 2010.

———. "BP Manager, Boss Both Ignored Warnings Before

Deepwater Horizon Blew, Panel Learns at Oil Spill Hearings." *New Orleans Times-Picayune*, August 26, 2010.

———. "5 Key Errors, Colossal Mechanical Failure Led to Fatal Gulf Oil Rig Blowout." *New Orleans Times-Picayune*, September 5, 2010.

Harkinson, Josh. "The Rig's on Fire! I Told You This Was Gonna Happen!" *Mother Jones*, June 7, 2010.

Junod, Tom. "Eleven Lives." *Esquire*, September 2010.

Leopold, Jason. "Whistleblower: BP Risks More Massive Catastrophes in Gulf." Truthout, April 30, 2010. http://www.truth-out .org/whistlelower-bps-other-offshore-drilling-project-gulf -vulnerable-catastrophe59027.

Lyall, Sarah. "In BP's Record, a History of Boldness and Costly Blunders." *New York Times*, July 12, 2010.

McKinley, James. "Documents Fill In Gaps in Narrative on Oil Rig Blast." *New York Times*, September 7, 2010.

National Academy of Engineering and National Research Council. *Interim Report on Causes of the* Deepwater Horizon *Oil Rig Blowout and Ways to Prevent Such Events*. Washington, D.C.: National Academies Press.

National Commission on the BP Deepwater Horizon Oil Spill and Offshore Drilling. *Master Presentation*. November 9, 2010.

Parsons, Paul. "Drilling Background." Energy Training Resources, June 29, 2010.

———. "The Macondo Well." Energy Training Resources, July 15, 2010.

Perry, David. "Re: Kenneth Abbott/BP Atlantis Threat to GOM Environment." Letter, Perry & Hass Attorneys at Law, May 27, 2009.

Resnick-Ault, Jessica. "BP Oil-Leak Estimate Doubled by U.S. Science Panel." *Bloomberg News*, June 11, 2010.

Robertson, Campbell. "Oil Leaking Underwater from Well in Rig Blast." *New York Times*, April 24, 2010.

60 Minutes. "Blowout: The Deepwater Horizon Disaster." CBS News, May 16, 2010.

Chapter 6: SAILING THE SLICK

Dragonfly Boatworks. "Jimmy Buffett S.W.A.T Boat to Aid Oil-Soaked Wildlife in Gulf." Press release, June 10, 2010.

Murtaugh, Dan. "Tar Balls Hit Baldwin." *Mobile Press-Register*, May 12, 2010.

Raines, Ben. "BP Buys Up Gulf Scientists for Legal Defense, Roiling Academic Community." *Mobile Press-Register*, July 16, 2010.

Chapter 7: OF EELS, WHALES, AND REPERCUSSIONS

Allen, Terry. "Gulf Dispersants: BP and Nalco Play Toxic Roulette." CorpWatch, July 19, 2010. http://www.corpwatch.org/article .php?id=15609.

Berger, Matthew. "Gulf of Mexico Oil Spill's 30-Year Legacy." IPS News, September 3, 2010. http://ipsnews.net/news.asp?idnews= 52714.

Biello, David. "Where Will the Deepwater Horizon Oil End Up?" *Scientific American*, May 19, 2010.

"Bon Secour Shrimpers Say Nets and Shrimp Covered with Oil, After Shrimping Trip off Louisiana Coast." *Local 15 News*, November 21, 2010.

Brown, David. "Study: Petroleum-Eating Microbes Significantly Reduced Gulf Oil Plume." *Washington Post*, August 24, 2010.

Brown, Matthew. "So Far, Most of Oil's Effects Felt in the Deep." *Houma Courier*, May 31, 2010.

Brown, Matthew, and Jason Dearen. "22-Mile Plume Nears Rich Waters." *Houma Courier*, May 29, 2010.

Brown, Matthew, and Ramit Plushnick-Masti. "Scientists Say Gulf Spill Is Altering Food Web." *Sun Herald*, July 15, 2010.

Burdeau, Cain. "Scientists Find Damage to Coral Near BP Well." *New York Times*, November 6, 2010.

Buskey, Nikki. "Reports of Underwater Oil Are Exaggerated, Officials Say." *Houma Courier*, May 18, 2010.

Chesapeake Bay Program. "American Eel." Bay Field Guide. http://www.chesapeakebay.net/american_eel.htm.

Dell'Amore, Christine. "'Sea Snot' Explosion Caused by Gulf Oil Spill?" *National Geographic News*, September 23, 2010.

Fahrenthold, David. "Scientists Question Government Team's Report of Shrinking Gulf Oil Spill." *Washington Post*, August 5, 2010.

Froomkin, Dan. "Researchers Found 40-Fold Increase in Carcinogenic Compounds in Gulf." *Huffington Post*, September 30, 2010. http://www.huffingtonpost.com/2010/09/30/researchers-find-heighten_n_745834.html.

Gillis, Justin. "Scientists Build Case for Undersea Plumes." *New York Times*, May 28, 2010.

Gillis, Justin, and John Collins Rudolph. "Gulf Oil Plume Is Not Breaking Down Fast, Research Says." *New York Times*, August 19, 2010.

Graham, William, et al. "Oil Carbon Entered the Coastal Planktonic Food Web During the Deepwater Horizon Oil Spill." *Environmental Research Letters*, October–December 2010.

Hazen, Terry, et al. "Deep-Sea Oil Plume Enriches Indigenous Oil-Degrading Bacteria." *Science*, October 8, 2010.

Joye, Samantha. "Where Has the Oil Gone?" *Gulf Oil Blog*, August 1, 2010. http://gulfblog.uga.edu/2010/08/where-has-the-oil-gone.

Juhasz, Antonia. *The Tyranny of Oil*. New York: William Morrow, 2008.

Keim, Brandon. "Gulf Coast May Be Permanently Changed by Oil Spill." *Wired*, May 5, 2010.

————. "Saving Fish Is Possible, Unless They're Past the Tipping Point." *Wired*, July 30, 2010.

Khan, Amina. "Oil Dispersant Effects Remain a Mystery." *Los Angeles Times*, September 4, 2010.

Kirkham, Chris. "Federal Leaders of Gulf of Mexico Oil Spill Response Report Only a Few Lingering Trouble Spots." *New Orleans Times-Picayune*, October 18, 2010.

"Laboratory Test Results Raise Concern over Gulf Seafood." *WFTV News*, November 22, 2010.

Lubchenko, Jane, et al. "BP Deepwater Horizon Oil Budget: What Happened to the Oil?" National Oceanic and Atmospheric Administration press release, August 2, 2010.

Maine Department of Marine Resources. "The Maine Eel and Elver Fishery." http://www.maine.gov/dmr/rm/eel.html.

Marshall, Bob. "Can Crabs Overcome Oil During the Peak Spawning Season?" *New Orleans Times-Picayune*, July 21, 2010.

Mulvaney, Kieran. "Save the Whales, Save the Poop." Discovery News, October 13, 2010. http://dsc.discovery.com/ads/ad_in terstitial_fill6.html?dest=http://news.discovery.com/earth/ save-the-whales-save-the-poop.html.

Niiler, Eric. "Gulf Oil Spill Fallout: How Bad Is It?" Discovery News, September 15, 2010. http://news.discovery.com/earth/ gulf-oil-spill-recovery.html.

Pennsylvania State University. "Scientists Discover Dying Corals, Creatures Near Gulf Oil Spill Site." Press release, November 5, 2010.

Philpot, Tom. "Chemical Dispersants Being Used in Gulf Clean-Up Are Potentially Toxic." Grist, May 6, 2010. http://www .grist.org/article/2010-05-06-use-of-toxic-chemical-disper sants-to-fight-the-oil-spill-a-murky.

Plushnick-Masti, Ramit. "'Gulf Weed' Could Be Spill Casualty." MSNBC, June 22, 2010. http://www.msnbc.msn.com/id/ 37855306/ns/us_news-environment.

Prosek, James. "Mystery Travelers." *National Geographic*, September 2010.

Raines, Ben. "Degraded Oil in Mississippi Sound Tests Positive for Dispersants, Says Lawyer." *Mobile Press-Register*, August 31, 2010.

———. "FDA's Standards for Gulf Seafood May Be Lower Than Those in Past Oil Spills." *Mobile Press-Register*, September 5, 2010.

———. " 'Shadow' of Oil Spill Seen in Gulf of Mexico Plankton." *Mobile Press-Register*, November 8, 2010.

Raloff, Janet. "Gases Dominate Gulf's Subsea Plumes." *Science News*, October 9, 2010.

Rudolf, John Collins. "Dead Coral Found Near Site of Gulf Oil Spill." *New York Times*, November 5, 2010.

———. "Deep Underwater, Oil Threatens Reefs." *New York Times*, June 1, 2010.

Tont, Sargun A. "Deep Scattering Layers: Patterns in the Pacific." *California Cooperative Oceanic Fisheries Investigations*, vol. 18, July 1, 1973–June 30, 1975.

"Scientists: Oil Droplets Speckle Gulf Floor, Evidence Seen That Oil Has Become Toxic to Critical Marine Life." *Underwater Times*, August 17, 2010.

Sheppard, Kate. "Why Is the EPA Letting BP Use Dirty Dispersants?" *Mother Jones*, May 19, 2010.

Sturgis, Sue. "Independent Tests Find Oil-Spill Contamination in Louisiana Oysters and Crabs." *Southern Studies*, August 31, 2010.

Valentine, David, et al. "Propane Respiration Jump-Starts Microbial Response to a Deep Oil Spill." *Science*, October 8, 2010.

Wang, Marian. "In Gulf Spill, BP Using Dispersants Banned in UK." ProPublica, May 18, 2010. http://www.propublica.org/blog/item/In-Gulf-Spill-BP-Using-Dispersants-Banned-in-UK.

———. "Scientists Dispute Government Stance on the Lingering Effects of Gulf Oil." ProPublica, August 17, 2010. http://www .propublica.org/blog/item/several-scientific-reports-cast -doubt-on-government-stance-on-gulf-oil.

Webster, Stephen C. "Multiple Independent Lab Tests Confirm Oil in Gulf Shrimp." Raw Story, November 10, 2010. http://www .rawstory.com/rs/2010/11/activist-lab-tests-show-dangerously -toxic-substances-present-gulf-shrimp.

"Where's The Oil? On the Gulf Floor, Scientists Say." Associated Press, September 13, 2010.

Whitty, Julia. "The BP Cover-Up." *Mother Jones*, August 10, 2010.

Chapter 8: THE LAST DAYS OF
ISLE DE JEAN CHARLES

Barry, Dan. "In Louisiana, a Sinking Island Wars with Water and the Government." *New York Times*, June 19, 2006.

Burdeau, Cain. "Spill Reinforces Oil Bad Will for Local American Indians." *Houma Courier*, May 18, 2010.

Buskey, Nikki. "Residents Unite to Save Land, Water." *Houma Courier*, June 3, 2010.

"Isle de Jean Charles Band of Biloxi-Chitimacha Indians." Biloxi-Chitimacha-Choctaw of Louisiana. http://www.biloxi-chiti macha.com/isle_de_jean_charles.htm.

Larson, Susan. "The Hurricane of 1856, Which Swept Across the Resort of Isle Derniere, Returns in Two New Books." *New Orleans Times-Picayune*, May 27, 2009.

McPhee, John. "Atchafalaya." *New Yorker*, February 23, 1987.

Philipp, Joshua. "BP Oil Spill Taking Toll on Local Indian Tribe." *Epoch Times*, October 31, 2010.

Saulny, Susan. "Holding Out, to Last Tiny Isle, as Cajun Land Sinks into Gulf." *New York Times*, August 24, 2008.

Sutter, John. "How the Gulf of Mexico Became the Nation's 'Toilet Bowl.'" CNN, July 27, 2010.

Tidwell, Mike. *Bayou Farewell*. New York: Vintage, 2003.

Woodruff, Bob, et al. "Louisianans Watch Native Land Sinking into Sea." *ABC News*, December 6, 2009.

Chapter 9: TEN THOUSAND CUTS

Boyce, Daniel, et al. "Global Phytoplankton Decline over the Past Century." *Nature,* July 29, 2010.

DeSantis, John. "Giant Spill Latest in Coast's Complicated Relationship with Oilfield." *Houma Courier*, May 16, 2010.

Donn, Jeff, and Mitch Weiss. "Gulf Awash in 27,000 Abandoned Wells." Associated Press. July 7, 2010.

Greenberg, Paul. "Tuna's End." *New York Times Magazine*, June 21, 2010.

Juhasz, Antonia. *The Tyranny of Oil*. New York: William Morrow, 2008.

"Marine Phytoplankton Declining: Striking Global Changes at the Base of the Marine Food Web Linked to Rising Ocean Temperatures." ScienceDaily, July 28, 2010. http://www.science daily.com/releases/2010/07/100728131705.htm.

Raines, Ben. "Gulf Rigs: Islands of Contamination." *Mobile Press-Register*, December 30, 2001.

Raines, Ben, and Bill Finch. "Rig Shrimp Test High for Mercury." *Mobile Press-Register*, January 27, 2002.

Robertson, Campbell. "Gulf of Mexico Has Long Been a Sink of Pollution." *New York Times*, July 29, 2010.

Rudolf, John Collins. "Will Gulf Fish Get a Break?" *New York Times*, May 11, 2010.

Schleifstein, Mark. "Mississippi River Pours as Much Dispersant into the Gulf of Mexico as BP." *New Orleans Times-Picayune*, August 5, 2010.

Seibert, Charles. "Watching Whales Watching Us." *New York Times Magazine,* July 12, 2009.

Weilgart, Linda. "Underwater Noise: Death Knell of Our Oceans?" TerraNature, November 7, 2005. http://www.terranature .org/oceanNoise_Weilgart.htm.

Whitty, Julia. "The BP Cover-Up." *Mother Jones,* August 10, 2010.

Wilson, Diane. "The BP Oil Gusher Is Just the Latest in a Long Line of Assaults on the Gulf of Mexico." Grist, May 28, 2010. http:// www.grist.org/article/2010-05-28-the-bp-oil-gusher-is-just -the-latest-in-a-long-line-of-assaults-/.

Chapter 10: PLACELESSNESS

Associated Press. "Widespread Oyster Deaths Found on Louisiana Reefs." *New Orleans Times-Picayune,* July 17, 2010.

Ball, Jeffrey. "Fresh Water Aimed at Oil Kills Oysters." *Wall Street Journal,* July 21, 2010.

Barry, Dan. "From a Gulf Oyster, a Domino Effect." *New York Times,* July 16, 2010.

Dow, Nicole. "Up to 90% of Oysters Dead in DMR's Reef Sample." *Sun Herald,* September 2, 2010.

Handwerk, Brian. "New Orleans Sinking Faster Than Thought, Satellites Find." National Geographic News, June 1, 2006. http://news.nationalgeographic.com/news/2006/06/060601 -new-orleans.html.

Houck, Oliver. "Can We Save New Orleans?" *Tulane Environmental Law Journal,* spring 2006.

Huffstutter, P. J., et al. "The Oyster Is Their World, But Oil Spill Threatens It." *Los Angeles Times,* July 18, 2010.

McPhee, John. "Atchafalaya." *New Yorker,* February 23, 1987.

Philipp, Joshua. "BP Oil Spill Taking Toll on Local Indian Tribe." *Epoch Times,* October 31, 2010.

Schmit, Julie. "Oil Spill's Trickledown Effect." *USA Today*, May 13, 2010.

State of Louisiana. "Office of Coastal Protection and Restoration Officials Open Additional Freshwater Diversions to Help Protect Coastal Wetlands from Oil Spill." Press release, May 7, 2010.

Taylor, Claire. "Barataria Bay 'Devastation.'" Daily World, August 1, 2010.

Chapter 11: BP Is My Copilot

"Amazon Defense Coalition: Court Filing: Chevron's Own Audits Prove Company Lied About Massive Pollution in Ecuador." BusinessWire. August 31, 2010. http://www.businesswire.com/news/home/20100831006022/en/Amazon-Defense-Coalition-Court-Filing-Chevron%E2%80%99s-Audits.

Angus, Ian. "The BP Oil Disaster: Blaming Individual Consumers for Capitalist Destruction." Global Research, September 13, 2010. http://www.globalresearch.ca/index.php?context=va&aid=21023.

Batker, David, et al. *Gaining Ground*. Tacoma, WA: Earth Economics, 2010.

Buskey, Nikki. "Coastal Parishes Get 'Pittance' in Offshore Revenues." *Houma Courier*, October 21, 2010.

Finch, Bill. "Gulf Spill Update: The Numbers Don't Lie." Cool Green Science, May 26, 2010. http://blog.nature.org/2010/05/gulf-spill-update-the-numbers-dont-lie.

Houck, Oliver. "Can We Save New Orleans?" *Tulane Environmental Law Journal*, spring 2006.

———. "Who Will Pay to Fix Louisiana?" *Nation*, June 24, 2010.

International Energy Agency. "Oil Market Report." June 10, 2010. http://www.edf.org/documents/11240_EDF%20Audobon%20NWF%20Common%20Ground%20White%20Paoer.pdf.

Klare, Michael. "A New Oil Rush Endangers the Gulf of Mexico

and the Planet." TomDispatch, May 18, 2010. http://www
.globalresearch.ca/index.php?context=va&aid=19268.

Krauss, Clifford, and John Broder. "Spotlight Shifts to Shallow-
Water Wells." *New York Times*, September 3, 2010.

Maass, Peter. *Crude World*. New York: Knopf, 2009.

Nossiter, Adam. "Far from Gulf, a Spill Scourge 5 Decades Old."
New York Times, June 16, 2010.

U.S. Energy Information Administration. "Crude Oil Production."
http://www.eia.doe.gov/dnav/pet/pet_crd_crpdn_adc_mb
blpd_a.htm.

Weber, Harry, and John Flesher. "World's Oil Thirst Leads to
Risks." *Houma Courier*, November 5, 2010.

Chapter 12: CREATING LAND AND OTHER MINOR MIRACLES

America's Wetland. "America's Wetland Foundation—Who We
Are." americaswetland.com/files/080410-AWF-WhoWeAre
FINALREV.pdf.

Batker, David, et al. *Gaining Ground*. Tacoma, WA: Earth Economics, 2010.

Environmental Defense Fund, National Audubon Society, and National Wildlife Federation. "Common Ground: A Shared Vision
for Restoring the Mississippi River Delta," July 28, 2010. http://
www.edf.org/documents/11240_EDF%20Audobon%20NWF
%20Common%20Ground%20White%20Paoer.pdf.

Houck, Oliver. "Who Will Pay to Fix Louisiana?" *Nation*, June 24,
2010.

Jacobsen, Rowan, and Michael Beck. "Where Oysters Grew on Trees."
New York Times, July 24, 2010.

Louisiana-Mississippi Gulf Coast Ecosystem Restoration Working
Group. "Roadmap for Restoring Ecosystem Resiliency and
Sustainability," March 2010.

Marshall, Bob. "BP Oil Spill Disaster Could End Up Working in Favor of Coastal Restoration." *New Orleans Times-Picayune*, August 22, 2010.

McCollam, Douglas. "Cleaning Up: The New Model." *New York Times*, November 4, 2010.

Schliefstein, Mark. "Coastal Restoration Trust Fund Idea Backed by America's Energy Coast." *New Orleans Times-Picayune*, September 21, 2010.

———. "Gulf Restoration Plan Should Be Home-Grown, EPA Administrator Lisa Jackson Says." *New Orleans Times-Picayune*, October 5, 2010.

———. "Missouri River Helped Build Louisiana Coast, But It Won't Help Restore It." *New Orleans Times-Picayune*, September 29, 2010.

U.S. Government Accountability Office. *Oil and Gas Royalties: A Comparison of the Share of Revenue Received from Oil and Gas Production by the Federal Government and Other Resource Owners.* May 1, 2007. http://www.gao.gov/htext/d07676r.html.

Chapter 13: THE MOST IMPORTANT RIVER YOU'VE NEVER HEARD OF

Burdeau, Cain. "Louisiana Sand Berms Are Not Stopping Much Oil from Gulf of Mexico Spill, EPA Says." *New Orleans Times-Picayune*, September 9, 2010.

Kirgan, Harlan. "Salt Dome Foes Keep Eye on Project Despite Its Removal from Department of Energy Budget." *Mississippi Press*, April 2, 2010.

Olsen, Ken. "Mississippi's Pearl: The Pascagoula." National Wildlife Federation, July 14, 2010. http://www.nwf.org/News-and-Magazines/National-Wildlife/News-and-Views/Archives/2010/The-Pascagoula.aspx.

SOURCES

Rudolf, John Collins. "Louisiana and Scientists Spar Over How to Stop Oil." *New York Times*, July 6, 2010.

Epilogue: THANKSGIVING

Finch, Bill. "We Are All a Part of the Life of the Gulf." *Mobile Press-Register*, November 25, 2010.

INDEX

and Gulf of Mexico, 21, 22–23, 25, 140–41

headwaters of, 21

levees of, 11, 25, 111, 118, 121–22, 156, 179, 187

navigability of, 118, 120

and New Orleans, 150, 151–52

St. Lawrence compared to, 24–25

soil carried by, 22–26, 121, 187

waste carried by, 141–42, 187–88

Mississippi River—Gulf Outlet Canal (MR. GO), 116, 153, 160

Monroe, James, 119

Morel, Brian, 46

mud-gas separator, 63

Napoléon Bonaparte, 119–20

Naquin, Jean Marie, 112

Native Americans, 29–30, 115

natural gas, 35, 47
flaring, 132–33
pipeline explosion, 178

Natural Resources Damage Assessment and Restoration, 78, 184

Nature Conservancy, 3, 28, 171–72

negative-pressure test, 55, 57, 58–61, 68

New Orleans
Cajuns in, 30
French Quarter in, 147–48, 203
geography of, 150–53
and the Mississippi, 150, 151–52
mystique of, 149, 166
oyster business in, 146–47, 153–61, 163–66, 203
and river plantations, 118
sinking, 152
as swamp city, 149, 151

tourists in, 148–50, 153

as trading port, 119

and War of 1812, 120

Niger Delta, oil in, 169

nitrified foam cement, 50–55, 58

NOAA (National Oceanic and Atmospheric Administration), 93–100

Obama, Barack, 40, 98, 183

offshore drilling, 35–36, 40
and environmental movement, 36–37
finding costs, 39, 42
royalties for, 168, 185–86
safety incidents in, 41, 140, 177
technology advances in, 36, 38–39

oil, 32–43, 47
as commodity, 174
consumption of, 38, 172–73
crude, 97, 102, 132–33, 168
deepwater era, 38, 39, 40
"elephant" reservoirs of, 37, 38, 39, 40
foreign sources of, 39
formation of, 34–35
lifting costs of, 39
offshore drilling for, 35–36
plumes of, 96, 97, 101
prices of, 39, 40, 174
and Resource Curse, 169
shallow-water production of, 38, 39
taxes on, 185

oil-eating microbes, 94–95, 96–97, 100–101

oil industry
air guns used by, 138–39
canals dug by, 18, 114–17, 138, 160–61
and habitat loss, 15, 117, 140

A NOTE ON THE AUTHOR

ROWAN JACOBSEN is the James Beard Award-winning author of *A Geography of Oysters*, *Fruitless Fall*, *The Living Shore*, and *American Terroir*. He has written about food, place, and the natural world for *Harper's*, *Newsweek*, *Eating Well*, and others, and his commentaries on the Gulf crisis have appeared in *Outside* magazine and the *New York Times* and on MSNBC. Jacobsen was raised in Florida and attended school on the Gulf Coast.